Death Penalty Decisions Of The United States Supreme Court

Maureen Harrison & Steve Gilbert
Editors

📖 **Excellent Books** 📖
Carlsbad, California

EXCELLENT BOOKS
Post Office Box 131322
Carlsbad, CA 92013-1322

Publisher's Cataloging in Publication Data

Death Penalty Decisions Of The United States Supreme Court/
  Maureen Harrison, Steve Gilbert, editors.
   p. cm.
Bibliography: p.

1. United States. Supreme Court.
I. Title. II. Harrison, Maureen. III. Gilbert, Steve.

KF8694.D34 2003   LC 2002110908
342.2 -dc20

ISBN 1-880780-24-0

Introduction

Excessive bail shall not be required, nor excessive fines imposed, nor cruel and unusual punishments be inflicted.
- The Eighth Amendment, December 15, 1791

The Founding Fathers wrote into the Bill of Rights a prohibition against the infliction of "cruel and unusual punishments." From that day to this the legal definition of what constitutes a "cruel and unusual punishment" has been left to the Justices of the United States Supreme Court.

The basic constitutionality of the death penalty was, for almost two hundred years, never in question. In the late 1800's, in the Court's first two Cruel and Unusual Punishment decisions, both in capital punishment cases, the Justices found that the Eighth Amendment allowed them to prohibit inhumane punishments. In 1878 the Court, while upholding the constitutionality of execution by firing squad, stated, *Punishments of torture . . . and all others in the same line of unnecessary cruelty, are forbidden by the [Eighth] Amendment to the Constitution.*[1] In 1890 the Court, while upholding the constitutionality of execution by electrocution, stated, *Punishments are cruel and unusual when they involve torture or lingering death; but the punishment of death is not cruel.*[2]

In the Courts next three Cruel and Unusual Punishment decisions - the first two non-capital punishment cases, and the third a capital punishment case - the Justices found the Eighth Amendment allowed them to prohibit excessive punishments. In 1903 the Court, in overturning a previous decision, found that a 10-year prison sentence for fraud was excessive punishment.[3] In 1910 the Court found a prison sentence of 10 years at hard labor in chains for falsifying public documents was again excessive. *Crime is repressed by penalties of just, not tormenting, severity.*[4] In 1947 the Court heard a convicted murderer's appeal to halt a second attempt to electrocute him after the first attempt had ended in a mechanical failure, *The traditional humanity of modern Anglo-American law forbids the infliction of unnecessary pain.*[5]

Finally, in 1958 the Justices, having established that the Eighth Amendment allowed them to prohibit inhumane punishments in capital cases and prohibit excessive punishments in non-capital cases heard an appeal that centered on the stripping of a native-born American's citizenship for desertion. The Court found that loss of citizenship, a permissible punishment in the past, was not necessarily permissible in the present, *The Eighth Amendment must draw its meaning from the evolving standards of decency that mark the progress of a maturing society.*[6]

These legal precedents, created over one hundred and eighty-one years, made the time ripe for a direct challenge to the constitutionality of the death penalty itself. The 1972 the *Furman v. Georgia* decision effectively voided 32 state death penalty statutes, thereby commuting the death sentences of 633 condemned prisoners.

Justice Benjamin Cardozo wrote this about some of the people whose personal legal problems have reached the United States Supreme Court - *The sordid controversies of litigants are the stuff out of which great and shining truths will ultimately be shaped.* The "sordid controversies" of people charged with criminal activities have many times found their way before the Supreme Court to become the "stuff out of which great and shining truths are shaped." These "great and shining truths," the Supreme Court's decisions on what constitutes criminal justice, have become binding legal precedents - the settled law of the land.

In its long history, the Supreme Court has issued thousands of individual decisions on Constitutional controversies. All have been important to the parties involved, but some - a significant few - are so important as to involve either the Constitutional rights or the Constitutional restrictions placed upon the rights of all Americans. These are Landmark Decisions, fundamentally altering the relationships of Americans to their institutions and to each other. This book deals with landmark decisions on the death penalty.

On the first Monday of each October, the United States Supreme Court begins a new Term. From all over the country, on all kinds of issues, and for all kinds of reasons, Americans bring controversies to the Court for a final disposition. Every year over five thousand requests for review of lower court decisions are received by the Court. Requests, called *petitions for certiorari*, come to the Court from the losing side in Federal Appeals Courts or State Supreme Courts. Four of the nine Justices must agree to a review. Review is accepted in only about four hundred cases each year. Once accepted, written arguments - briefs, pro and con - are submitted to the Court by both the petitioner (the losing side appealing the lower court's decision against them) and the respondent (the winning side defending the lower court's decision for them). Interested parties, called *amici curiae* (friends of the Court), may be permitted to submit briefs in support of either side. After all submitted briefs are reviewed by the Justices, public oral arguments are heard by the Court. Ordinarily the opposing sides, the petitioner and the respondent, are given thirty minutes of oral argument. The Justices, at their discretion, may interrupt at any time to require further explanations, to pose hypothetical questions, or to make observations. Twice a week, on Wednesdays and Fridays, the Justices meet alone in conference to discuss each case and vote on its outcome. They may affirm [let stand] or reverse [change the outcome of], in whole or in part, the decisions of the lower courts from which these appeals have come. One Justice, voting in the majority, will be selected to write the majority opinion. Others may join in the majority opinion, write their own concurring opinion, write their own dissenting opinion, or join in another's concurrence or dissent. Drafts of the majority, concurring, and dissenting opinions circulate among the Justices, and are redrafted and recirculated until a consensus is reached and a decision is announced. It is the majority opinion as finally issued by the Supreme Court that stands as the law of the land. All other Courts, Federal and State, are bound by Supreme Court precedent. The official legal texts of these decisions are published in the five hundred-plus volumes of *U.S. Reports*.

Judge Learned Hand wrote - *The language of the law must not be foreign to the ears of those who are to obey it.* The Landmark Decisions presented in this book are carefully edited, plain-English versions of the official legal texts issued by the Supreme Court in *United States Reports*. We, as editors, have made every effort to replace esoteric legalese with understandable everyday English without damaging the original decisions. Edited out are long alpha-numeric legal citations and wordy wrangles over points of proce-dure. Edited in are definitions (*writ of habeas corpus* = an order from a judge to bring a person to court), translations (*certiorari* = the decision of the Court to review a case), identifications (petitioner = the individual appealing a lower court's decision; respondent = the individual defending the lower court's deci-sion), and explanations (where the case originated, how it got to the court, and who all the parties involved were).

You will find in *Death Penalty Decisions* the majority opinion of the Court as expressed by the Justice chosen to speak for the Court. Preceding each edited decision, we note where the complete deci-sion can be found. The bibliography provides a list of further reading on the issues before the Court.

Chief Justice John Marshall wrote that a Supreme Court decision "comes home in its effect to every man's fireside; it passes on his property, his reputation, his life, his all." We entered into editing books on landmark Supreme Court decisions because we, like you, and your family and friends, must obey, under penalty of law, these decisions. It stands to reason that if we owe our obedi-ence to what the Supreme Court decides, then we owe it to our-selves to know what they have written, not second-hand, but for ourselves. You don't have to wait to have your rights read to you - you can read them for yourself.

M.H.& S.G.

[1] *Wilkerson v. Utah*, 99 U.S. (1878)
[2] *In re Kemmler*, 136 U.S. (1890)
[3] *Howard v. Fleming*, 191 U.S. (1903)
[4] *Weems v. United States*, 217 U.S. (1910)
[5] *Francis v. Resweber*, 329 U.S. (1947)
[6] *Trop v. Dulles*, 356 U.S. (1958)

Table Of Contents

Disproportionate Punishment
Enmund v. Florida
57

American criminal law has long considered a defendant's intention - and therefore his moral guilt - to be critical to the degree of [his] criminal culpability.

- Justice Byron White (1982)

Executing The Insane
Ford v. Wainwright
71

The Eighth Amendment prohibits the State from inflicting the penalty of death upon a prisoner who is insane.

- Justice Thurgood Marshall (1986)

Executing Minors I
Thompson v. Oklahoma
85

We are not persuaded that the imposition of the death penalty for offenses committed by persons under sixteen years of age has made, or can be expected to make, any measurable contribution to the goals that capital punishment is intended to achieve.

- Justice John Paul Stevens (1988)

Executing Minors II
Stanford v. Kentucky
95

We discern neither a historical nor a modern societal consensus forbidding the imposition of capital punishment on any person who murders at sixteen or seventeen years of age.

- Justice Antonin Scalia (1989)

Cruel And Unusual Punishment I
Furman v. Georgia

Does the imposition and carrying out of the death penalty constitute cruel and unusual punishment in violation of the Eighth and Fourteenth Amendments? **- Per Curiam Decision**

In mid-1972, 633 condemned prisoners were awaiting execution on the death rows of 32 States. One of them was a thirty-year-old African-American named William Henry Furman. Furman had been charged with murder in connection with a botched robbery. He was tried, found guilty, and, on September 26, 1968, the jury (which under Georgia law had full discretion to impose a life or death sentence) voted to put William Henry Furman to death. After the Georgia Supreme Court affirmed his death sentence, Furman appealed to the United States Supreme Court on the grounds that as a poor person and a racial minority, the death penalty imposed upon him was arbitrary and discriminatory - a violation of his Eighth [Cruel and Unusual Punishment] and Fourteenth [Equal Protection] rights. "Cruel and unusual punishment," Furman argued, should not only mean that no execution could be inhuman or barbarous but also that no execution decision could be racially arbitrary or discriminatory. "Equal Protection," Furman argued, should extend to equal punishment for a crime based on the severity of the crime and not on the race of the criminal. The Supreme Court granted a review of his death sentence limited to the following question, *Does the imposition and carrying out of the death penalty in the case of William Henry Furman constitute cruel and unusual punishment in violation of the Eighth and Fourteenth Amendments?*

On June 29, 1972 the 5-4 decision of the United States Supreme Court was announced *per curiam* [by the entire Court]. Associate Justice William O. Douglas filed a concurrence, which follows the majority decision.

The *Furman* Court

Chief Justice Warren Burger
Appointed Chief Justice by President Nixon
Served 1969 - 1986

Associate Justice William O. Douglas
Appointed by President Franklin Roosevelt
Served 1939 - 1975

Associate Justice William Brennan
Appointed by President Eisenhower
Served 1956 - 1990

Associate Justice Potter Stewart
Appointed by President Eisenhower
Served 1958 - 1981

Associate Justice Byron White
Appointed by President Kennedy
Served 1962 - 1993

Associate Justice Thurgood Marshall
Appointed by President Lyndon Johnson
Served 1967 - 1991

Associate Justice Harry Blackmun
Appointed by President Nixon
Served 1970 - 1994

Associate Justice Lewis Powell
Appointed by President Nixon
Served 1971 - 1987

Associate Justice William Rehnquist
Appointed by President Nixon
Served 1971 -

The legal text of *Furman v. Georgia* can be found in Volume 408 of *United States Reports*. Our edited text follows.

FURMAN v. GEORGIA
June 29, 1972

PER CURIAM [by the entire Court]: Petitioner [one who brings an appeal to court] was convicted of murder in Georgia and was sentenced to death pursuant to Georgia [law]. . . . [Review] was granted limited to the following question: "Does the imposition and carrying out of the death penalty . . . constitute cruel and unusual punishment in violation of the Eighth and Fourteenth Amendments?" The Court holds that the imposition and carrying out of the death penalty . . . constitutes cruel and unusual punishment in violation of the Eighth and Fourteenth Amendments. The judgment [of the Georgia Supreme Court] . . . is therefore reversed insofar as it leaves undisturbed the death sentence imposed, and the [case is] remanded [sent back to the lower court] for further proceedings. So ordered.

JUSTICE WILLIAM O. DOUGLAS, concurring: . . . [T]he death penalty was imposed [on William Henry Furman] for murder. . . . [T]he determination of whether the penalty should be death or a lighter punishment was left by the State to the discretion of . . . the jury. [This review is] limited to the question whether the imposition and execution of the death penalty constitute "cruel and unusual punishment" within the meaning of the Eighth Amendment as applied to the States by the Fourteenth. I vote to vacate [overturn] the judgment, believing that the exaction of the death penalty does violate the Eighth and Fourteenth Amendments.

That the requirements of due process ban cruel and unusual punishment is now settled. It is also settled that the proscription of cruel and unusual punishments forbids the judicial imposition of them as well as their imposition by the legislature.

Congressman [First] Bingham, in proposing the Fourteenth Amendment, maintained that "the privileges or immunities of citizens of the United States," as protected by the Fourteenth Amendment, included protection against "cruel and unusual punishments": "[M]any instances of State injustice and oppression have already occurred in the State legislation of this Union, of flagrant violations of the guarantied privileges of citizens of the United States, for which the national Government furnished and could furnish by law no remedy whatever. Contrary to the express letter of your Constitution, 'cruel and unusual punishments' have been inflicted under State laws within this Union upon citizens not only for crimes committed, but for sacred duty done, for which and against which the Government of the United States had provided no remedy, and could provide none."

Whether the privileges and immunities route is followed or the due process route, the result is the same.

It has been assumed in our decisions that punishment by death is not cruel, unless the manner of execution can be said to be inhuman and barbarous. It is also said in our opinions that the proscription of cruel and unusual punishments "is not fastened to the obsolete, but may acquire meaning as public opinion becomes enlightened by a humane justice." [T]he Eighth Amendment "must draw its meaning from the evolving standards of decency that mark the progress of a maturing society."

The generality of a law inflicting capital punishment is one thing. What may be said of the validity of a law on the books and what may be done with the law in its application do, or may, lead to quite different conclusions.

It would seem to be incontestable that the death penalty inflicted on one defendant is "unusual" if it discriminates against him by reason of his race, religion, wealth, social position, or class, or if it is imposed under a procedure that gives room for the play of such prejudices.

There is evidence that the provision of the English Bill of Rights of 1689, from which the language of the Eighth Amendment was taken, was concerned primarily with selective or irregular application of harsh penalties, and that its aim was to forbid arbitrary and discriminatory penalties of a severe nature,

"Following the Norman conquest of England in 1066, the old system of penalties, which ensured equality between crime and punishment, suddenly disappeared. By the time systematic judicial records were kept, its demise was almost complete. With the exception of certain grave crimes for which the punishment was death or outlawry, the arbitrary fine was replaced by a discretionary amercement. Although amercement's discretionary character allowed the circumstances of each case to be taken into account, and the level of cash penalties to be decreased or increased accordingly, the amercement presented an opportunity for excessive or oppressive fines.

"The problem of excessive amercements became so prevalent that three chapters of the Magna Carta were devoted to their regulation. . . ."

The English Bill of Rights, enacted December 16, 1689, stated that "excessive bail ought not to be required, nor excessive fines imposed, nor cruel and unusual punishments inflicted." These were the words chosen for our Eighth Amendment. A like provision had been in Virginia's Constitution of 1776, and in the constitutions of seven other States. The Northwest Ordinance, enacted under the Articles of Confederation, included a prohibition of cruel and unusual punishments. But the debates of the First Congress on the Bill of Rights throw little light on its intended meaning. All that appears is the following:

"Mr. Smith, of South Carolina, objected to the words 'nor cruel and unusual punishments,' the import of them being too indefinite.

"Mr. Livermore: The clause seems to express a great deal of humanity, on which account I have no objection to it; but, as it seems to have no meaning in it, I do not think it necessary. What is meant by the term excessive bail? Who are to be the judges? What is understood by excessive fines? It lies with the court to determine. No cruel and unusual punishment is to be inflicted; it is sometimes necessary to hang a man, villains often deserve whipping, and perhaps having their ears cut off; but are we in future to be prevented from inflicting these punishments because they are cruel? If a more lenient mode of correcting vice and deterring others from the commission of it could be invented, it would be very prudent in the Legislature to adopt it; but until we have some security that this will be done, we ought not to be restrained from making necessary laws by any declaration of this kind."

The words "cruel and unusual" certainly include penalties that are barbaric. But the words, at least when read in light of the English proscription against selective and irregular use of penalties, suggest that it is "cruel and unusual" to apply the death penalty - or any other penalty - selectively to minorities whose numbers are few, who are outcasts of society, and who are unpopular, but whom society is willing to see suffer though it would not countenance general application of the same penalty across the board. [As] Judge Tuttle, indeed, made abundantly clear . . . solitary confinement may at times be "cruel and unusual" punishment.

The Court in *McGautha v. California* noted that in this country, there was almost from the beginning a "rebellion against the common law rule imposing a mandatory death sentence on all convicted murderers." The first attempted remedy was to restrict the death penalty to defined offenses such as "premeditated" murder. But juries "took the law into their own hands," and refused to convict on the capital offense.

"In order to meet the problem of jury nullification, legislatures did not try, as before, to refine further the definition of capital homicides. Instead they adopted the method of forthrightly granting juries the discretion which they had been exercising in fact."

The Court concluded: In light of history, experience, and the present limitations of human knowledge, we find it quite impossible to say that committing to the untrammeled discretion of the jury the power to pronounce life or death in capital cases is offensive to anything in the Constitution.

The Court refused to find constitutional dimensions in the argument that those who exercise their discretion to send a person to death should be given standards by which that discretion should be exercised.

A recent witness at the Hearings before the House Committee on the Judiciary stated,

> "Any penalty, a fine, imprisonment or the death penalty could be unfairly or unjustly applied. The vice in this case is not in the·penalty, but in the process by which it is inflicted. It is unfair to inflict unequal penalties on equally guilty parties, or on any innocent parties, *regardless of what the penalty is.*"

But those who advance that argument overlook *McGautha.*

. . . . Juries (or judges, as the case may be) have practically untrammeled discretion to let an accused live or insist that he die.

Mr. Justice Field, dissenting in *O'Neil v. Vermont* said, "The State may, indeed, make the drinking of one drop of liquor an offense to be punished by imprisonment, but it would be an unheard-of cruelty if it should count the drops in a single glass and make thereby a thousand offenses, and thus extend the punishment for drinking the single glass of liquor to an imprisonment of almost indefinite duration." What the legislature may not do for all classes uniformly and systematically a judge or jury may not do for a class that prejudice sets apart from the community.

There is increasing recognition of the fact that the basic theme of equal protection is implicit in "cruel and unusual" punishments. "A penalty . . . should be considered 'unusually' imposed if it is administered arbitrarily or discriminatorily." The same authors add that "[t]he extreme rarity with which applicable death penalty provisions are put to use raises a strong inference of arbitrariness." The President's Commission on Law Enforcement and Administration of Justice recently concluded,

"Finally, there is evidence that the imposition of the death sentence and the exercise of dispensing power by the courts and the executive follow discriminatory patterns. The death sentence is disproportionately imposed, and carried out on the poor, the Negro, and the members of unpopular groups."

A study of capital cases in Texas from 1924 to 1968 reached the following conclusions:

"Application of the death penalty is unequal: most of those executed were poor, young, and ignorant.

"Seventy-five of the 460 cases involved codefendants, who, under Texas law, were given separate trials. In several instances where a white and a Negro were co-defendants, the white was sentenced to life imprisonment or a term of years, and the Negro was given the death penalty.

"Another ethnic disparity is found in the type of sentence imposed for rape. The Negro convicted of rape is far more likely to get the death penalty than a term sentence, whereas whites and Latins are far more likely to get a term sentence than the death penalty."

Warden Lewis E. Lawes of Sing Sing said,

"Not only does capital punishment fail in its justification, but no punishment could be invented with so many inherent defects. It is an unequal punishment in the way it is applied to the rich and to the poor. The defendant of wealth and position never goes to the electric chair or to the gallows. Juries do not intentionally favor the rich, the law is theoretically impartial, but the defendant with ample means is able to have his case presented with every favorable aspect, while the poor defendant often has a lawyer assigned by the court. Sometimes such assignment is considered part of political patronage; usually the lawyer assigned has had no experience whatever in a capital case."

Former Attorney General Ramsey Clark has said, "It is the poor, the sick, the ignorant, the powerless and the hated who are executed." One searches our chronicles in vain for the execution of any member of the affluent strata of this society. The Leopolds and Loebs are given prison terms, not sentenced to death.

. . . . Furman, a black, killed a householder while seeking to enter the home at night. Furman shot the deceased through a closed door. He was 26 years old and had finished the sixth grade in school. Pending trial, he was committed to the Georgia Central State Hospital for a psychiatric examination on his plea of insanity tendered by court-appointed counsel. The superintendent reported that a unanimous staff diagnostic conference had concluded "that this patient should retain his present diagnosis of Mental Deficiency, Mild to Moderate, with Psychotic Episodes associated with Convulsive Disorder." The physicians agreed that "at present the patient is not psychotic, but he is not capable of cooperating with his counsel in the preparation of his defense"; and the staff believed "that he is in need of further psychiatric hospitalization and treatment."

Later, the superintendent reported that the staff diagnosis was Mental Deficiency, Mild to Moderate, with Psychotic Episodes associated with Convulsive Disorder. He concluded, however, that Furman was "not psychotic at present, knows right from wrong and is able to cooperate with his counsel in preparing his defense."

. . . . We cannot say from facts disclosed in these records that [Furman was] sentenced to death because [he was] black. Yet our task is not restricted to an effort to divine what motives impelled [the] death penalt[y]. Rather, we deal with a system of law and of justice that leaves to the uncontrolled discretion of judges or juries the determination whether defendants committing these crimes should die or be imprisoned. Under these laws, no standards govern the selection of the penalty. People live or die, dependent on the whim of one man or of twelve.

. . . . Those who wrote the Eighth Amendment knew what price their forebears had paid for a system based not on equal justice, but on discrimination. In those days, the target was not the blacks or the poor, but the dissenters, those who opposed absolutism in government, who struggled for a parliamentary regime, and who opposed governments' recurring efforts to foist a particular religion on the people. But the tool of capital punishment was used with vengeance against the opposition and those unpopular with the regime. One cannot read this history without realizing that the desire for equality was reflected in the ban against "cruel and unusual punishments" contained in the Eighth Amendment.

In a Nation committed to equal protection of the laws there is no permissible "caste" aspect of law enforcement. Yet we know that the discretion of judges and juries in imposing the death penalty enables the penalty to be selectively applied, feeding prejudices against the accused if he is poor and despised, and lacking political clout, or if he is a member of a suspect or unpopular minority, and saving those who by social position may be in a more protected position. In ancient Hindu law, a Brahman was exempt from capital punishment, and, under that law, "[g]enerally, in the law books, punishment increased in severity as social status diminished." We have, I fear, taken in practice the same position, partially as a result of making the death penalty discretionary and partially as a result of the ability of the rich to purchase the services of the most respected and most resourceful legal talent in the Nation.

The high service rendered by the "cruel and unusual" punishment clause of the Eighth Amendment is to require legislatures to write penal laws that are evenhanded, nonselective, and nonarbitrary, and to require judges to see to it that general laws are not applied sparsely, selectively, and spottily to unpopular groups.

A law that stated that anyone making more than $50,000 would be exempt from the death penalty would plainly fall, as would a law that in terms said that blacks, those who never went beyond the fifth grade in school, those who made less than $3,000 a year, or those who were unpopular or unstable should be the only people executed. A law which, in the overall view, reaches that result in practice has no more sanctity than a law which in terms provides the same.

Thus, these discretionary statutes are unconstitutional in their operation. They are pregnant with discrimination, and discrimination is an ingredient not compatible with the idea of equal protection of the laws that is implicit in the ban on "cruel and unusual" punishments.

Any law which is nondiscriminatory on its face may be applied in such a way as to violate the Equal Protection Clause of the Fourteenth Amendment. Such conceivably might be the fate of a mandatory death penalty, where equal or lesser sentences were imposed on the elite, a harsher one on the minorities or members of the lower castes. Whether a mandatory death penalty would otherwise be constitutional is a question I do not reach.

I concur in the judgments of the Court.

Cruel And Unusual Punishment II
Gregg v. Georgia

No longer can a jury wantonly and freakishly impose a penalty of death.
- Justice Potter Stewart

On June 29, 1972, in *Furman v. Georgia*, the United States Supreme Court struck down Georgia's death penalty statute (and by extension the similar death penalty statues of thirty-one other states) as prejudicial and arbitrary, a violation of the Constitution's prohibition against cruel and unusual punishment.

The five-justice majority was made up of two justices voting that any imposition of the death penalty constituted cruel and unusual punishment, and three justices voting that only the prejudicial and arbitrary imposition of the death penalty constituted cruel and unusual punishment. Four justices voted that no imposition of the death penalty constituted cruel and unusual punishment.

Many State Legislatures, including the Georgia Legislature, immediately amended their death penalty statutes to remove the unconstitutional prejudicial and arbitrary elements.

On November 24, 1973 Troy Leon Gregg was arrested by Gwinnett County (Georgia) Police on a charge of multiple murders. Tried and convicted of the murders, Gregg was sentenced to death under Georgia's new death penalty statute. On appeal, the Georgia Supreme Court upheld Gregg's death sentence. Gregg appealed to the United States Supreme Court to overturn his death sentence on the grounds that any imposition of the death penalty was unconstitutional, a violation of the Constitution's prohibition against cruel and unusual punishment.

On July 2, 1976 the 7-2 decision of the Supreme Court was announced by Associate Justice Potter Stewart.

The *Gregg* Court

Chief Justice Warren Burger
Appointed Chief Justice by President Nixon
Served 1969 - 1986

Associate Justice William O. Douglas
Appointed by President Franklin Roosevelt
Served 1939 - 1975

Associate Justice William Brennan
Appointed by President Eisenhower
Served 1956 - 1990

Associate Justice Potter Stewart
Appointed by President Eisenhower
Served 1958 - 1981

Associate Justice Byron White
Appointed by President Kennedy
Served 1962 - 1993

Associate Justice Thurgood Marshall
Appointed by President Lyndon Johnson
Served 1967 - 1991

Associate Justice Harry Blackmun
Appointed by President Nixon
Served 1970 - 1994

Associate Justice Lewis Powell
Appointed by President Nixon
Served 1971 - 1987

Associate Justice William Rehnquist
Appointed by President Nixon
Served 1971 -

The legal text of *Gregg v. Georgia* can be found in volume 428 of *United States Reports*. Our edited text follows.

GREGG v. GEORGIA
July 2, 1976

JUSTICE POTTER STEWART: The issue in this case is whether the imposition of the sentence of death for the crime of murder under the law of Georgia violates the Eighth and Fourteenth Amendments.

The petitioner [one who brings an appeal to the court], Troy Gregg, was charged with committing armed robbery and murder. In accordance with Georgia procedure in capital cases, the trial was in two stages, a guilt stage and a sentencing stage. The evidence at the guilt trial established that, on November 21, 1973, [Gregg] and a traveling companion, Floyd Allen, while hitchhiking . . . were picked up by Fred Simmons and Bob Moore. . . . The next morning the bodies of Simmons and Moore were discovered in a ditch.

On November 23, after reading about the shootings in an Atlanta newspaper, [a witness] communicated with the Gwinnett County police and related information concerning . . . the victims, including a description of the car. The next afternoon, [Gregg] and Allen, while in Simmons' car, were arrested in Asheville, N.C. In the search incident to the arrest a .25-caliber pistol, later shown to be that used to kill Simmons and Moore, was found in [Gregg's] pocket. After receiving the warnings required by *Miranda v. Arizona*, and signing a written waiver of his rights, [Gregg] signed a statement in which he admitted shooting, then robbing Simmons and Moore. He justified the slayings on grounds of self-defense.

The trial judge submitted the murder charges to the jury on both felony-murder and nonfelony-murder theories. He also instructed on the issue of self-defense, but declined to instruct on manslaughter. He submitted the robbery case to the jury on both an armed robbery theory and on the lesser included offense of robbery by intimidation. The jury found [Gregg] guilty of two counts of armed robbery and two counts of murder.

At the penalty stage, which took place before the same jury, neither the prosecutor nor [Gregg]'s lawyer offered any additional evidence. Both counsel, however, made lengthy arguments dealing generally with the propriety of capital punishment under the circumstances and with the weight of the evidence of guilt. The trial judge instructed the jury that it could recommend either a death sentence or a life prison sentence on each count. The judge further charged the jury that, in determining what sentence was appropriate, the jury was free to consider the facts and circumstances, if any, presented by the parties in mitigation or aggravation.

Finally, the judge instructed the jury that it "would not be authorized to consider [imposing] the penalty of death" unless it first found beyond a reasonable doubt one of these aggravating circumstances:

"*One.* That the offense of murder was committed while the offender was engaged in the commission of two other capital felonies, to wit, the armed robbery of [Simmons and Moore].

"*Two.* That the offender committed the offense of murder for the purpose of receiving money and the automobile described in the indictment.

"*Three.* The offense of murder was outrageously and wantonly vile, horrible and inhuman, in that [it] involved the depravity of [the] mind of the defendant."

Finding the first and second of these circumstances, the jury returned verdicts of death on each count.

The Supreme Court of Georgia affirmed the convictions and the imposition of the death sentences for murder. After reviewing the trial transcript and the record, including the evidence, and comparing the evidence and sentence in similar cases in accordance with the requirements of Georgia law, the court concluded that, considering the nature of the crime and the defendant, the sentences of death had not resulted from prejudice or any other arbitrary factor and were not excessive or disproportionate to the penalty applied in similar cases. The death sentences imposed for armed robbery, however, were vacated on the grounds that the death penalty had rarely been imposed in Georgia for that offense, and that the jury improperly considered the murders as aggravating circumstances for the robberies after having considered the armed robberies as aggravating circumstances for the murders.

We granted the petitioner's application for [a review] limited to his challenge to the imposition of the death sentences in this case as "cruel and unusual" punishment in violation of the Eighth and the Fourteenth Amendments.

. . . . We address initially the basic contention that the punishment of death for the crime of murder is, under all circumstances, "cruel and unusual" in violation of the Eighth and Fourteenth Amendments of the Constitution. . . .

The Court, on a number of occasions, has both assumed and asserted the constitutionality of capital punishment. In several cases, that assumption provided a necessary foundation for the decision, as the Court was asked to decide whether a particular method of carrying out a capital sentence would be allowed to stand under the Eighth Amendment. But until *Furman v. Georgia,* the Court never confronted squarely the fundamental claim that the punishment of death always, regardless of the enormity of the offense or the procedure followed in imposing the sentence, is cruel and unusual punishment in violation of the Constitution. Although this issue was presented and addressed in *Furman,* it was not resolved by the Court. Four Justices would have held that capital punishment is not unconstitutional per se; two Justices would have reached the opposite conclusion; and three Justices, while agreeing that the statutes then before the Court were invalid as applied, left open the question whether such punishment may ever be imposed. We now hold that the punishment of death does not invariably violate the Constitution.

The history of the prohibition of "cruel and unusual" punishment already has been reviewed at length. The phrase first appeared in the English Bill of Rights of 1689, which was drafted by Parliament at the accession of William and Mary. The English version appears to have been directed against punishments unauthorized by statute and beyond the jurisdiction of the sentencing court, as well as those disproportionate to the offense involved. "The American draftsmen, who adopted the English phrasing in drafting the Eighth Amendment, were primarily concerned, however, with proscribing 'tortures' and other 'barbarous' methods of punishment."

In the earliest cases raising Eighth Amendment claims, the Court focused on particular methods of execution to determine whether they were too cruel to pass constitutional muster. The constitutionality of the sentence of death itself was not at issue, and the criterion used to evaluate the mode of execution was its similarity to "torture" and other "barbarous" methods.

But the Court has not confined the prohibition embodied in the Eighth Amendment to "barbarous" methods that were generally outlawed in the 18th century. Instead, the Amendment has been interpreted in a flexible and dynamic manner. The Court early recognized that "a principle to be vital must be capable of wider application than the mischief which gave it birth." Thus, the Clause forbidding "cruel and unusual" punishments "is not fastened to the obsolete, but may acquire meaning as public opinion becomes enlightened by a humane justice."

. . . . The imposition of the death penalty for the crime of murder has a long history of acceptance both in the United States and in England. The common law rule imposed a mandatory death sentence on all convicted murderers. And the penalty continued to be used into the 20th century by most American States, although the breadth of the common law rule was diminished, initially by narrowing the class of murders to be punished by death and subsequently by widespread adoption of laws expressly granting juries the discretion to recommend mercy.

It is apparent from the text of the Constitution itself that the existence of capital punishment was accepted by the Framers. At the time the Eighth Amendment was ratified, capital punishment was a common sanction in every State. Indeed, the First Congress of the United States enacted legislation providing death as the penalty for specified crimes. The Fifth Amendment, adopted at the same time as the Eighth, contemplated the continued existence of the capital sanction by imposing certain limits on the prosecution of capital cases:

"No person shall be held to answer for a capital, or otherwise infamous crime, unless on a presentment or indictment of a Grand Jury . . . ; nor shall any person be subject for the same offense to be twice put in jeopardy of life or limb; . . . nor be deprived of life, liberty, or property, without due process of law. . . ."

And the Fourteenth Amendment, adopted over three-quarters of a century later, similarly contemplates the existence of the capital sanction in providing that no State shall deprive any person of "life, liberty, or property" without due process of law.

. . . . Four years ago, the petitioners in *Furman* and its companion cases predicated their argument primarily upon the asserted proposition that standards of decency had evolved to the point where capital punishment no longer could be tolerated. The petitioners in those cases said, in effect, that the evolutionary process had come to an end, and that standards of decency required that the Eighth Amendment be construed finally as prohibiting capital punishment for any crime, regardless of its depravity and impact on society. This view was accepted by two Justices. Three other Justices were unwilling to go so far; focusing on the procedures by which convicted defendants were selected for the death penalty, rather than on the actual punishment inflicted, they joined in the conclusion that the statutes before the Court were constitutionally invalid.

The petitioners in the capital cases before the Court today renew the "standards of decency" argument, but developments during the four years since *Furman* have undercut substantially the assumptions upon which their argument rested. Despite the continuing debate, dating back to the 19th century, over the morality and utility of capital punishment, it is now evident that a large proportion of American society continues to regard it as an appropriate and necessary criminal sanction.

The most marked indication of society's endorsement of the death penalty for murder is the legislative response to *Furman*. The legislatures of at least 35 States have enacted new statutes that provide for the death penalty for at least some crimes that result in the death of another person. . . .

The death penalty is said to serve two principal social purposes: retribution and deterrence of capital crimes by prospective offenders.

In part, capital punishment is an expression of society's moral outrage at particularly offensive conduct. This function may be unappealing to many, but it is essential in an ordered society that asks its citizens to rely on legal processes, rather than self-help, to vindicate their wrongs.

"The instinct for retribution is part of the nature of man, and channeling that instinct in the administration of criminal justice serves an important purpose in promoting the stability of a society governed by law. When people begin to believe that organized society is unwilling or unable to impose upon criminal offenders the punishment they deserve, then there are sown the seeds of anarchy - of self-help, vigilante justice, and lynch law.

"Retribution is no longer the dominant objective of the criminal law, but neither is it a forbidden objective, nor one inconsistent with our respect for the dignity of men. Indeed, the decision that capital punishment may be the appropriate sanction in extreme cases is an expression of the community's belief that certain crimes are themselves so grievous an affront to humanity that the only adequate response may be the penalty of death."

Although some of the studies suggest that the death penalty may not function as a significantly greater deterrent than lesser penalties, there is no convincing empirical evidence either supporting or refuting this view. We may nevertheless assume safely that there are murderers, such as those who act in passion, for whom the threat of death has little or no deterrent effect. But for many others, the death penalty undoubtedly is a significant deterrent. There are carefully contemplated murders, such as murder for hire, where the possible penalty of death may well enter into the cold calculus that precedes the decision to act. And there are some categories of murder, such as murder by a life prisoner, where other sanctions may not be adequate.

The value of capital punishment as a deterrent of crime is a complex factual issue the resolution of which properly rests with the legislatures, which can evaluate the results of statistical studies in terms of their own local conditions and with a flexibility of approach that is not available to the courts. Indeed, many of the post-*Furman* statutes reflect just such a responsible effort to define those crimes and those criminals for which capital punishment is most probably an effective deterrent.

. . . . The cruelty against which the Constitution protects a convicted man is cruelty inherent in the method of punishment, not the necessary suffering involved in any method employed to extinguish life humanely.

In sum, we cannot say that the judgment of the Georgia Legislature that capital punishment may be necessary in some cases is clearly wrong.

Finally, we must consider whether the punishment of death is disproportionate in relation to the crime for which it is imposed. There is no question that death, as a punishment, is unique in its severity and irrevocability. When a defendant's life is at stake, the Court has been particularly sensitive to insure that every safeguard is observed. But we are concerned here only with the imposition of capital punishment for the crime of murder, and, when a life has been taken deliberately by the offender, we cannot say that the punishment is invariably disproportionate to the crime. It is an extreme sanction, suitable to the most extreme of crimes.

We hold that the death penalty is not a form of punishment that may never be imposed, regardless of the circumstances of the offense, regardless of the character of the offender, and regardless of the procedure followed in reaching the decision to impose it.

. . . . The basic concern of *Furman* centered on those defendants who were being condemned to death capriciously and arbitrarily. Under the procedures before the Court in that case, sentencing authorities were not directed to give attention to the nature or circumstances of the crime committed or to the character or record of the defendant. Left unguided, juries imposed the death sentence in a way that could only be called freakish. The new Georgia sentencing procedures, by contrast, focus the jury's attention on the particularized nature of the crime and the particularized characteristics of the individual defendant. While the jury is permitted to consider any aggravating or mitigating circumstances, it must find and identify at least one statutory aggravating factor before it may impose a penalty of death. In this way, the jury's discretion is channeled. No longer can a jury wantonly and freakishly impose the death sentence; it is always circumscribed by the legislative guidelines. In addition, the review function of the Supreme Court of Georgia affords additional assurance that the concerns that prompted our decision in *Furman* are not present to any significant degree in the Georgia procedure applied here.

For the reasons expressed in this opinion, we hold that the statutory system under which Gregg was sentenced to death does not violate the Constitution. Accordingly, the judgment of the Georgia Supreme Court is affirmed. It is so ordered.

Mandatory Death Sentences
Woodson v. North Carolina

The history of mandatory death penalty statutes in the United States reveals that the practice of sentencing to death all persons convicted of a particular offense has been rejected as unduly harsh and unworkably rigid.
- Justice Potter Stewart

In 1972's *Furman* decision, the Supreme Court struck down the death penalty statute of Georgia, and by extension all similarly-drawn death penalty statutes, as prejudicial and arbitrary violations of the Eighth Amendment's prohibition against cruel and unusual punishment.

In an attempt to comply with the *Furman* decision, eleven states, including North Carolina, modified their capital punishment statutes to make the death penalty mandatory for all persons convicted of first-degree murder.

Mandatory death sentences had long been abandoned by all fifty states and their sudden reappearance, as a replacement for pre-*Furman* jury discretion, was viewed by death penalty opponents as a disguised attempt to reinstate the death penalty.

On June 3, 1974 in Dunn, North Carolina, Tyrone Woodson and three accomplices murdered E-Z Shop clerk Shirley Whittington Butler. Woodson was tried and convicted of first-degree murder. Under North Carolina's new mandatory death statute, Woodson received an automatic death sentence.

The Supreme Court, which had never before ruled on the constitutionality of mandatory death penalty statutes, agreed to hear Woodson's appeal.

On July 2, 1976 the 5-4 decision of the Supreme Court was announced by Associate Justice Potter Stewart.

The *Woodson* Court

Chief Justice Warren Burger
Appointed Chief Justice by President Nixon
Served 1969 - 1986

Associate Justice William O. Douglas
Appointed by President Franklin Roosevelt
Served 1939 - 1975

Associate Justice William Brennan
Appointed by President Eisenhower
Served 1956 - 1990

Associate Justice Potter Stewart
Appointed by President Eisenhower
Served 1958 - 1981

Associate Justice Byron White
Appointed by President Kennedy
Served 1962 - 1993

Associate Justice Thurgood Marshall
Appointed by President Lyndon Johnson
Served 1967 - 1991

Associate Justice Harry Blackmun
Appointed by President Nixon
Served 1970 - 1994

Associate Justice Lewis Powell
Appointed by President Nixon
Served 1971 - 1987

Associate Justice William Rehnquist
Appointed by President Nixon
Served 1971 -

The legal text of *Woodson v. North Carolina* can be found in volume 428 of *United States Reports*. Our edited text follows.

WOODSON v. NORTH CAROLINA
July 2, 1976

JUSTICE POTTER STEWART: The question in this case is whether the imposition of a death sentence for the crime of first-degree murder under the law of North Carolina violates the Eighth and Fourteenth Amendments.

The petitioners [those who bring an appeal to the court] were convicted of first-degree murder as the result of their participation in an armed robbery of a convenience food store, in the course of which the cashier was killed and a customer was seriously wounded. There were four participants in the robbery: the petitioners James Tyrone Woodson and Luby Waxton and two others, Leonard Tucker and Johnnie Lee Carroll. At the . . . trial [of Woodson and Waxton] Tucker and Carroll testified for the prosecution after having been permitted to plead guilty to lesser offenses; [Woodson and Waxton] testified to plead [their] own defense.

The evidence for the prosecution established that the four men had been discussing a possible robbery for some time. On the fatal day Woodson had been drinking heavily. About 9:30 p. m., Waxton and Tucker came to the trailer where Woodson was staying. When Woodson came out of the trailer, Waxton struck him in the face and threatened to kill him in an effort to make him sober up and come along on the robbery. The three proceeded to Waxton's trailer where they met Carroll. Waxton armed himself with a nickel-plated derringer, and Tucker handed Woodson a rifle. The four then set out by automobile to rob the store. Upon arriving at their destination, Tucker and Waxton went into the store, while Carroll and Woodson remained in the car as lookouts. Once inside the store, Tucker purchased a package of cigarettes from the woman cashier. Waxton then also asked for a package of cigarettes, but as the cashier approached him he pulled the derringer out of his hip pocket and fatally shot her at point-blank range. Waxton then took the money tray from the cash register and gave it to Tucker, who carried it out of the store, pushing past an entering customer as he reached the door.

After he was outside, Tucker heard a second shot from inside the store, and shortly thereafter Waxton emerged, carrying a handful of paper money. Tucker and Waxton got in the car and the four drove away.

[Woodson and Waxton's] testimony agreed in large part with this version of the circumstances of the robbery. It differed diametrically in one important respect: Waxton claimed that he never had a gun, and that Tucker had shot both the cashier and the customer.

During the trial Waxton asked to be allowed to plead guilty to the same lesser offenses to which Tucker had pleaded guilty, but the solicitor refused to accept the pleas. Woodson, by contrast, maintained throughout the trial that he had been coerced by Waxton, that he was therefore innocent, and that he would not consider pleading guilty to any offense.

[Woodson and Waxton] were found guilty on all charges, and, as was required by statute, sentenced to death. The Supreme Court of North Carolina affirmed [upheld]. We granted certiorari [agreed to hear the case], to consider whether the imposition of the death penalties in this case comports with the Eighth and Fourteenth Amendments to the United States Constitution.

[Woodson and Waxton] argue that the imposition of the death penalty under any circumstances is cruel and unusual punishment in violation of the Eighth and Fourteenth Amendments. We reject this argument for the reasons stated today in *Gregg v. Georgia.*

At the time of this Court's decision in *Furman v. Georgia,* North Carolina law provided that in cases of first-degree murder, the jury in its unbridled discretion could choose whether the convicted defendant [one charged with a crime] should be sentenced to death or to life imprisonment. After the *Furman* decision, the Supreme Court of North Carolina in *State v. Waddell,* held unconstitutional the provision of the death penalty statute that gave the jury the option of returning a verdict of guilty without capital punishment [the death penalty], but held further that this provision was severable [capable of being separate] so that the statute survived as a mandatory death penalty law.

The North Carolina General Assembly in 1974 followed the court's lead and enacted a new statute that was essentially unchanged from the old one except that it made the death penalty mandatory. The statute now reads as follows:

"Murder in the first and second degree defined; punishment. - A murder which shall be perpetrated by means of poison, lying in wait, imprisonment, starving, torture, or by any other kind of willful, deliberate and premeditated killing, or which shall be committed in the perpetration or attempt to perpetrate any arson, rape, robbery, kidnapping, burglary or other felony, shall be deemed to be murder in the first degree and shall be punished with death. All other kinds of murder shall be deemed murder in the second degree, and shall be punished by imprisonment for a term of not less than two years nor more than life imprisonment in the State's prison."

It was under this statute that [Woodson and Waxton], who committed their crime on June 3, 1974, were tried, convicted, and sentenced to death.

North Carolina, unlike Florida, Georgia, and Texas, has thus responded to the *Furman* decision by making death the mandatory sentence for all persons convicted of first-degree murder. In ruling on the constitutionality of the sentences imposed on [Woodson and Waxton] under this North Carolina statute, the Court now addresses for the first time the question whether a death sentence returned pursuant to a law imposing a mandatory death penalty for a broad category of homicidal offenses constitutes cruel and unusual punishment within the meaning of the Eighth and Fourteenth Amendments. The issue, like that explored in *Furman*, involves the procedure employed by the State to select persons for the unique and irreversible penalty of death.

The Eighth Amendment stands to assure that the State's power to punish is "exercised within the limits of civilized standards."

. . . . [We] begin by sketching the history of mandatory death penalty statutes in the United States. At the time the Eighth Amendment was adopted in 1791, the States uniformly followed the common-law [law based on usage and custom] practice of making death the exclusive and mandatory sentence for certain specified offenses. Although the range of capital offenses in the American Colonies was quite limited in comparison to the more than 200 offenses then punishable by death in England, the Colonies at the time of the Revolution imposed death sentences on all persons convicted of any of a considerable number of crimes, typically including at a minimum, murder, treason, piracy, arson, rape, robbery, burglary, and sodomy. As at common law, all homicides that were not involuntary, provoked, justified, or excused constituted murder and were automatically punished by death. Almost from the outset jurors reacted unfavorably to the harshness of mandatory death sentences. The States initially responded to this expression of public dissatisfaction with mandatory statutes by limiting the classes of capital offenses.

This reform, however, left unresolved the problem posed by the not infrequent refusal of juries to convict murderers rather than subject them to automatic death sentences. In 1794, Pennsylvania attempted to alleviate the undue severity of the law by confining the mandatory death penalty to "murder of the first degree" encompassing all "wilful, deliberate and premeditated" killings. Other jurisdictions, including Virginia and Ohio, soon enacted similar measures, and within a generation the practice spread to most of the States.

Despite the broad acceptance of the division of murder into degrees, the reform proved to be an unsatisfactory means of identifying persons appropriately punishable by death. Although its failure was due in part to the amorphous nature of the controlling concepts of willfulness, deliberateness, and premeditation, a more fundamental weakness of the reform soon became apparent. Juries continued to find the death penalty inappropriate in a significant number of first-degree murder cases and refused to return guilty verdicts for that crime.

The inadequacy of distinguishing between murderers solely on the basis of legislative criteria narrowing the definition of the capital offense led the States to grant juries sentencing discretion in capital cases. Tennessee in 1838, followed by Alabama in 1841, and Louisiana in 1846, were the first States to abandon mandatory death sentences in favor of discretionary death penalty statutes. This flexibility remedied the harshness of mandatory statutes by permitting the jury to respond to mitigating [reducing] factors by withholding the death penalty. By the turn of the century, 23 States and the Federal Government had made death sentences discretionary for first-degree murder and other capital offenses. During the next two decades 14 additional States replaced their mandatory death penalty statutes. Thus, by the end of World War I, all but eight States, Hawaii, and the District of Columbia either had adopted discretionary death penalty schemes or abolished the death penalty altogether. By 1963, all of these remaining jurisdictions had replaced their automatic death penalty statutes with discretionary jury sentencing.

The history of mandatory death penalty statutes in the United States thus reveals that the practice of sentencing to death all persons convicted of a particular offense has been rejected as unduly harsh and unworkably rigid. The two crucial indicators of evolving standards of decency respecting the imposition of punishment in our society - jury determinations and legislative enactments - both point conclusively to the repudiation of automatic death sentences. At least since the Revolution, American jurors have, with some regularity, disregarded their oaths and refused to convict defendants where a death sentence was the automatic consequence of a guilty verdict. As we have seen, the initial movement to reduce the number of capital offenses and to separate murder into degrees was prompted in part by the reaction of jurors as well as by reformers who objected to the imposition of death as the penalty for any crime. Nineteenth century journalists, statesmen, and jurists repeatedly observed that jurors were often deterred from convicting palpably guilty men of first-degree murder under mandatory statutes. Thereafter, continuing evidence of jury reluctance to convict persons of capital offenses in mandatory death penalty jurisdictions resulted in legislative authorization of discretionary jury sentencing - by Congress for federal crimes in 1897, by North Carolina in 1949, and by Congress for the District of Columbia in 1962.

. . . . [L]egislative measures adopted by the people's chosen representatives weigh heavily in ascertaining contemporary standards of decency. The consistent course charted by the state legislatures and by Congress since the middle of the past century demonstrates that the aversion of jurors to mandatory death penalty statutes is shared by society at large.

Still further evidence of the incompatibility of mandatory death penalties with contemporary values is provided by the results of jury sentencing under discretionary statutes. In *Witherspoon v. Illinois*, the Court observed that "one of the most important functions any jury can perform" in exercising its discretion to choose "between life imprisonment and capital punishment" is "to maintain a link between contemporary community values and the penal system." Various studies indicate that even in first-degree murder cases juries with sentencing discretion do not impose the death penalty "with any great frequency." The actions of sentencing juries suggest that under contemporary standards of decency death is viewed as an inappropriate punishment for a substantial portion of convicted first-degree murderers.

Although the Court has never ruled on the constitutionality of mandatory death penalty statutes, on several occasions dating back to 1899 it has commented upon our society's aversion to automatic death sentences. In *Winston v. United States*, the Court noted that the "hardship of punishing with death every crime coming within the definition of murder at common law, and the reluctance of jurors to concur in a capital conviction, have induced American legislatures, in modern times, to allow some cases of murder to be punished by imprisonment, instead of by death." Fifty years after *Winston*, the Court underscored the marked transformation in our attitudes toward mandatory sentences:

"The belief no longer prevails that every offense in a like legal category calls for an identical punishment without regard to the past life and habits of a particular offender. This whole country has traveled far from the period in which the death sentence was an automatic and commonplace result of convictions. . . ."

More recently, the Court in *McGautha v. California* detailed the evolution of discretionary imposition of death sentences in this country, prompted by what it termed the American "rebellion against the common-law rule imposing a mandatory death sentence on all convicted murderers." Perhaps the one important factor about evolving social values regarding capital punishment upon which the Members of the *Furman* Court agreed was the accuracy of *McGautha's* assessment of our Nation's rejection of mandatory death sentences. Justice Blackmun, for example, emphasized that legislation requiring an automatic death sentence for specified crimes would be "regressive and of an antique mold" and would mark a return to a "point in our criminology [passed beyond] long ago." The Chief Justice, speaking for the four dissenting Justices in *Furman*, discussed the question of mandatory death sentences at some length:

"I had thought that nothing was clearer in history, as we noted in *McGautha* one year ago, than the American abhorrence of 'the common-law rule imposing a mandatory death sentence on all convicted murderers.' As the concurring opinion of Justice Marshall shows, the 19th century movement away from mandatory death sentences marked an enlightened introduction of flexibility into the sentencing process. It recognized that individual culpability is not always measured by the category of the crime committed. This change in sentencing practice was greeted by the Court as a humanizing development."

Although it seems beyond dispute that, at the time of the *Furman* decision in 1972, mandatory death penalty statutes had been renounced by American juries and legislatures, there remains the question whether the mandatory statutes adopted by North Carolina and a number of other States following *Furman* evince a sudden reversal of societal values regarding the imposition of capital punishment. In view of the persistent and unswerving legislative rejection of mandatory death penalty statutes beginning in 1838 and continuing for more than 130 years until *Furman*, it seems evident that the post-*Furman* enactments reflect attempts by the States to retain the death penalty in a form consistent with the Constitution, rather than a renewed societal acceptance of mandatory death sentencing. The fact that some States have adopted mandatory measures following *Furman* while others have legislated standards to guide jury discretion appears attributable to diverse readings of this Court's multi-opinioned decision in that case.

A brief examination of the background of the current North Carolina statute serves to reaffirm our assessment of its limited utility as an indicator of contemporary values regarding mandatory death sentences. Before 1949, North Carolina imposed a mandatory death sentence on any person convicted of rape or first-degree murder. That year, a study commission created by the state legislature recommended that juries be granted discretion to recommend life sentences in all capital cases:

> "We propose that a recommendation of mercy by the jury in capital cases automatically carry with it a life sentence. Only three other states now have the mandatory death penalty and we believe its retention will be definitely harmful. Quite frequently, juries refuse to convict for rape or first degree murder because, from all the circumstances, they do not believe the defendant, although guilty, should suffer death. The result is that verdicts are returned hardly in harmony with evidence. Our proposal is already in effect in respect to the crimes of burglary and arson. There is much testimony that it has proved beneficial in such cases. We think the law can now be broadened to include all capital crimes."

The 1949 session of the General Assembly of North Carolina adopted the proposed modifications of its rape and murder statutes. Although in subsequent years numerous bills were introduced in the legislature to limit further or abolish the death penalty in North Carolina, they were rejected as were two 1969 proposals to return to mandatory death sentences for all capital offenses.

. . . [W]hen the Supreme Court of North Carolina analyzed the constitutionality of the State's death penalty statute following this Court's decision in *Furman,* it severed the 1949 proviso authorizing jury sentencing discretion and held that "the remainder of the statute with death as the mandatory punishment . . . remains in full force and effect." The North Carolina General Assembly then followed the course found constitutional in *Waddell* and enacted a first-degree murder provision identical to the mandatory statute in operation prior to the authorization of jury discretion. The State's brief [a written statement of one's position] in this case relates that the legislature sought to remove "all sentencing discretion [so that] there could be no successful *Furman* based attack on the North Carolina statute."

It is now well established that the Eighth Amendment draws much of its meaning from "the evolving standards of decency that mark the progress of a maturing society." . . . [O]ne of the most significant developments in our society's treatment of capital punishment has been the rejection of the common-law practice of inexorably imposing a death sentence upon every person convicted of a specified offense. North Carolina's mandatory death penalty statute for first-degree murder departs markedly from contemporary standards respecting the imposition of the punishment of death and thus cannot be applied consistently with the Eighth and Fourteenth Amendments' requirement that the State's power to punish "be exercised within the limits of civilized standards."

A separate deficiency of North Carolina's mandatory death sentence statute is its failure to provide a constitutionally tolerable response to *Furman*'s rejection of unbridled jury discretion in the imposition of capital sentences. Central to the limited holding in *Furman* was the conviction that the vesting of standardless sentencing power in the jury violated the Eighth and Fourteenth Amendments. It is argued that North Carolina has remedied the inadequacies of the death penalty statutes held unconstitutional in *Furman* by withdrawing all sentencing discretion from juries in capital cases. But when one considers the long and consistent American experience with the death penalty in first-degree murder cases, it becomes evident that mandatory statutes enacted in response to *Furman* have simply papered over the problem of unguided and unchecked jury discretion.

. . . . [T]here is general agreement that American juries have persistently refused to convict a significant portion of persons charged with first-degree murder of that offense under mandatory death penalty statutes. The North Carolina study commission reported that juries in that State "[q]uite frequently" were deterred from rendering guilty verdicts of first-degree murder because of the enormity of the sentence automatically imposed. Moreover, as a matter of historic fact, juries operating under discretionary sentencing statutes have consistently returned death sentences in only a minority of first-degree murder cases. In view of the historic record, it is only reasonable to assume that many juries under mandatory statutes will continue to consider the grave consequences of a conviction in reaching a verdict. North Carolina's mandatory death penalty statute provides no standards to guide the jury in its inevitable exercise of the power to determine which first-degree murderers shall live and which shall die. And there is no way under the North Carolina law for the judiciary to check arbitrary and capricious exercise of that power through a review of death sentences. Instead of rationalizing the sentencing process, a mandatory scheme may well exacerbate the problem identified in *Furman* by resting the penalty determination on the particular jury's willingness to act lawlessly. While a mandatory death penalty statute may reasonably be expected to increase the number of persons sentenced to death, it does not fulfill *Furman*'s basic requirement by replacing arbitrary and wanton jury discretion with objective standards to guide, regularize, and make rationally reviewable the process for imposing a sentence of death.

A third constitutional shortcoming of the North Carolina statute is its failure to allow the particularized consideration of relevant aspects of the character and record of each convicted defendant before the imposition upon him of a sentence of death. In *Furman*, members of the Court acknowledged what cannot fairly be denied - that death is a punishment different from all other sanctions in kind rather than degree. A process that accords no significance to relevant facets of the character and record of the individual offender or the circumstances of the particular offense excludes from consideration in fixing the ultimate punishment of death the possibility of compassionate or mitigating factors stemming from the diverse frailties of humankind. It treats all persons convicted of a designated offense not as uniquely individual human beings, but as members of a faceless, undifferentiated mass to be subjected to the blind infliction of the penalty of death.

This Court has previously recognized that "[f]or the determination of sentences, justice generally requires consideration of more than the particular acts by which the crime was committed and that there be taken into account the circumstances of the offense together with the character and propensities of the offender." Consideration of both the offender and the offense in order to arrive at a just and appropriate sentence has been viewed as a progressive and humanizing development. While the prevailing practice of individualizing sentencing determinations generally reflects simply enlightened policy rather than a constitutional imperative, we believe that in capital cases the fundamental respect for humanity underlying the Eighth Amendment, requires consideration of the character and record of the individual offender and the circumstances of the particular offense as a constitutionally indispensable part of the process of inflicting the penalty of death.

This conclusion rests squarely on the predicate that the penalty of death is qualitatively different from a sentence of imprisonment, however long. Death, in its finality, differs more from life imprisonment than a 100-year prison term difference from one of only a year or two. Because of that qualitative difference, there is a corresponding difference in the need for reliability in the determination that death is the appropriate punishment in a specific case.

For the reasons stated, we conclude that the death sentences imposed upon [Woodson and Waxton] under North Carolina's mandatory death sentence statute violated the Eighth and Fourteenth Amendments and therefore must be set aside [reversed]. The judgment of the Supreme Court of North Carolina is reversed insofar as it upheld the death sentences imposed upon [Woodson and Waxton], and the case is remanded [returned to the lower court] for further proceedings not inconsistent with this opinion. It is so ordered.

Excessive Punishment
Coker v. Georgia

We have the abiding conviction that the death penalty, which is unique in its severity and irrevocability, is an excessive penalty for the rapist.

- Justice Byron White

Prior to the 1972 *Furman* decision, which invalidated the capital punishment statutes of thirty-two states, sixteen of those states had authorized the death penalty not only for murder but for rape as well. By mid-1974, after all sixteen death-for-rape states had re-drafted their death penalty statutes to comply with *Furman*, only one state - Georgia - still punished rape with death. Under the Georgia death-for-rape statute, the jury, in the penalty phase of the trial, had to find the convicted rapist had committed the crime under aggravating circumstances.

On September 2, 1974 in Waycross, Georgia, Ehrlich Anthony Coker, a serial rapist and murderer then serving three consecutive life sentences, escaped from a Georgia prison, and, while on the run, robbed and raped sixteen-year-old Elnita Carver. Apprehended soon thereafter, Coker was tried and convicted for armed robbery, for which a jury sentenced him to a life sentence, and rape, for which a jury, finding aggravating circumstances, sentenced him to death.

The Georgia Supreme Court, which had previously rejected the appeals of four other convicted rapists sentenced to death, upheld Coker's rape conviction and the death sentence. Coker appealed to the U.S. Supreme Court on the grounds that the death sentence imposed on him for rape was a disproportionate punishment for his crime and so a violation of the Eighth Amendment's prohibition on cruel and unusual punishment.

On June 29, 1977 the 6-3 decision of the Supreme Court was announced by Associate Justice Byron White.

The *Coker* Court

Chief Justice Warren Burger
Appointed Chief Justice by President Nixon
Served 1969 - 1986

Associate Justice William Brennan
Appointed by President Eisenhower
Served 1956 - 1990

Associate Justice Potter Stewart
Appointed by President Eisenhower
Served 1958 - 1981

Associate Justice Byron White
Appointed by President Kennedy
Served 1962 - 1993

Associate Justice Thurgood Marshall
Appointed by President Lyndon Johnson
Served 1967 - 1991

Associate Justice Harry Blackmun
Appointed by President Nixon
Served 1970 - 1994

Associate Justice Lewis Powell
Appointed by President Nixon
Served 1971 - 1987

Associate Justice William Rehnquist
Appointed by President Nixon
Served 1971 -

Associate Justice John Paul Stevens
Appointed by President Ford
Served 1975 -

The legal text of *Coker v. Georgia* can be found in volume 438 of
United States Reports. Our edited text follows.

COKER v. GEORGIA
June 29, 1977

JUSTICE BYRON WHITE: Georgia [law] provides that "[a] person convicted of rape shall be punished by death or by imprisonment for life, or by imprisonment for not less than one nor more than 20 years." Punishment is determined by a jury in a separate sentencing proceeding in which at least one of the statutory aggravating [tending to add to the offense] circumstances must be found before the death penalty may be imposed. Petitioner [person bringing an appeal to court] [Ehrlich] Coker was convicted of rape and sentenced to death. Both the conviction and the sentence were affirmed [upheld] by the Georgia Supreme Court. Coker was granted a writ of certiorari [order allowing a court hearing], limited to the single claim, rejected by the Georgia court, that the punishment of death for rape violates the Eighth Amendment, which proscribes [prohibits] "cruel and unusual punishments" and which must be observed by the States as well as the Federal Government.

While serving various sentences for murder, rape, kidnapping, and aggravated assault, [Coker] escaped from the Ware Correctional Institution near Waycross, Georgia, on September 2, 1974. At approximately 11 o'clock that night, [Coker] entered the house of Allen and Elnita Carver through an unlocked kitchen door. Threatening the couple with a "board," he tied up Mr. Carver in the bathroom, obtained a knife from the kitchen, and took Mr. Carver's money and the keys to the family car. Brandishing the knife and saying "you know what's going to happen to you if you try anything, don't you," Coker then raped Mrs. Carver. Soon thereafter, [Coker] drove away in the Carver car, taking Mrs. Carver with him. Mr. Carver, freeing himself, notified the police; and not long thereafter [Coker] was apprehended. Mrs. Carver was unharmed.

[Coker] was charged with escape, armed robbery, motor vehicle theft, kidnapping, and rape. Counsel was appointed to represent him. Having been found competent to stand trial, he was tried. The jury returned a verdict of guilty, rejecting his general plea of insanity. A sentencing hearing was then conducted. . . . The jury was instructed that it could consider as aggravating circumstances whether the rape had been committed by a person with a prior record of conviction for a capital felony [a crime which may be punished by the death penalty] and whether the rape had been committed in the course of committing another capital felony, namely, the armed robbery of Allen Carver. The court also instructed . . . that even if aggravating circumstances were present, the death penalty need not be imposed if the jury found they were outweighed by mitigating circumstances, that is, circumstances not constituting justification or excuse for the offense in question, "but which, in fairness and mercy, may be considered as extenuating or reducing the degree" of moral culpability or punishment. The jury's verdict on the rape count was death by electrocution. Both aggravating circumstances on which the court instructed were found to be present by the jury.

. . . . It is now settled that the death penalty is not invariably cruel and unusual punishment within the meaning of the Eighth Amendment; it is not inherently barbaric or an unacceptable mode of punishment for crime; neither is it always disproportionate to the crime for which it is imposed. . . .

In sustaining [upholding] the imposition of the death penalty in *Gregg [v. Furman]* , however, the Court firmly embraced the holdings and dicta [opinions which are not binding] from prior cases, to the effect that the Eighth Amendment bars not only those punishments that are "barbaric" but also those that are "excessive" in relation to the crime committed. Under *Gregg*, a punishment is "excessive" and unconstitutional if it (1) makes no measurable contribution to acceptable goals of punishment and hence is nothing more than the purposeless and needless imposition of pain and suffering; or (2) is grossly out of proportion to the severity of the crime. A punishment might fail the test on either ground. Furthermore, these Eighth Amendment judgments should not be, or appear to be, merely the subjective views of individual Justices; judgment should be informed by objective factors to the maximum possible extent. To this end, attention must be given to the public attitudes concerning a particular sentence - history and precedent, legislative attitudes, and the response of juries reflected in their sentencing decisions are to be consulted. In *Gregg*, after giving due regard to such sources, the Court's judgment was that the death penalty for deliberate murder was neither the purposeless imposition of severe punishment nor a punishment grossly disproportionate to the crime. But the Court reserved [postponed] the question of the constitutionality of the death penalty when imposed for other crimes.

That question, with respect to rape of an adult woman, is now before us. We have concluded that a sentence of death is grossly disproportionate and excessive punishment for the crime of rape and is therefore forbidden by the Eighth Amendment as cruel and unusual punishment.

As advised by recent cases, we seek guidance in history and from the objective evidence of the country's present judgment concerning the acceptability of death as a penalty for rape of an adult woman. At no time in the last 50 years have a majority of the States authorized death as a punishment for rape. In 1925, 18 States, the District of Columbia, and the Federal Government authorized capital punishment for the rape of an adult female. By 1971 just prior to the decision in *Furman v. Georgia*, that number had declined, but not substantially, to 16 States plus the Federal Government. *Furman* then invalidated most of the capital punishment statutes in this country, including the rape statutes, because, among other reasons, of the manner in which the death penalty was imposed and utilized under those laws.

With their death penalty statutes for the most part invalidated, the States were faced with the choice of enacting modified capital punishment laws in an attempt to satisfy the requirements of *Furman* or of being satisfied with life imprisonment as the ultimate punishment for any offense. Thirty-five States immediately reinstituted the death penalty for at least limited kinds of crime. This public judgment as to the acceptability of capital punishment, evidenced by the immediate, post-*Furman* legislative reaction in a large majority of the States, heavily influenced the Court to sustain the death penalty for murder in *Gregg v. Georgia*.

But if the "most marked indication of society's endorsement of the death penalty for murder is the legislative response to *Furman*," it should also be a telling datum [a given thing] that the public judgment with respect to rape, as reflected in the statutes providing the punishment for that crime, has been dramatically different. In reviving death penalty laws to satisfy *Furman*'s mandate, none of the States that had not previously authorized death for rape chose to include rape among capital felonies. Of the 16 States in which rape had been a capital offense, only three provided the death penalty for rape of an adult woman in their revised statutes - Georgia, North Carolina, and Louisiana. In the latter two States, the death penalty was mandatory for those found guilty, and those laws were invalidated by *Woodson [v. North Carolina]* and *Roberts [v. Louisiana]*. When Louisiana and North Carolina, responding to those decisions, again revised their capital punishment laws, they re-enacted the death penalty for murder but not for rape; none of the seven other legislatures that to our knowledge have amended or replaced their death penalty statutes since July 2, 1976, including four States (in addition to Louisiana and North Carolina) that had authorized the death sentence for rape prior to 1972 and had reacted to *Furman* with mandatory statutes, included rape among the crimes for which death was an authorized punishment.

Georgia argues that 11 of the 16 States that authorized death for rape in 1972 attempted to comply with Furman by enacting arguably mandatory death penalty legislation and that it is very likely that, aside from Louisiana and North Carolina, these States simply chose to eliminate rape as a capital offense rather than to require death for each and every instance of rape. The argument is not without force; but 4 of the 16 States did not take the mandatory course and also did not continue rape of an adult woman as a capital offense. Further, as we have indicated, the legislatures of 6 of the 11 arguably mandatory States have revised their death penalty laws since *Woodson* and *Roberts* without enacting a new death penalty for rape. And this is to say nothing of 19 other States that enacted nonmandatory, post-*Furman* statutes and chose not to sentence rapists to death.

It should be noted that Florida, Mississippi, and Tennessee also authorized the death penalty in some rape cases, but only where the victim was a child and the rapist an adult. The Tennessee statute has since been invalidated because the death sentence was mandatory. The upshot is that Georgia is the sole jurisdiction in the United States at the present time that authorizes a sentence of death when the rape victim is an adult woman, and only two other jurisdictions provide capital punishment when the victim is a child.

The current judgment with respect to the death penalty for rape is not wholly unanimous among state legislatures, but it obviously weighs very heavily on the side of rejecting capital punishment as a suitable penalty for raping an adult woman.

It was also observed in *Gregg* that "[t]he jury . . . is a significant and reliable objective index of contemporary values because it is so directly involved," and that it is thus important to look to the sentencing decisions that juries have made in the course of assessing whether capital punishment is an appropriate penalty for the crime being tried. Of course, the jury's judgment is meaningful only where the jury has an appropriate measure of choice as to whether the death penalty is to be imposed. As far as execution for rape is concerned, this is now true only in Georgia and in Florida; and in the latter State, capital punishment is authorized only for the rape of children.

According to the factual submissions in this Court, out of all rape convictions in Georgia since 1973 - and that total number has not been tendered - 63 cases had been reviewed by the Georgia Supreme Court as of the time of oral argument; and of these, 6 involved a death sentence, 1 of which was set aside, leaving 5 convicted rapists now under sentence of death in the State of Georgia. Georgia juries have thus sentenced rapists to death six times since 1973. This obviously is not a negligible number; and the State argues that as a practical matter juries simply reserve the extreme sanction for extreme cases of rape and that recent experience surely does not prove that jurors consider the death penalty to be a disproportionate punishment for every conceivable instance of rape, no matter how aggravated. Nevertheless, it is true that in the vast majority of cases, at least 9 out of 10, juries have not imposed the death sentence.

These recent events evidencing the attitude of state legislatures and sentencing juries do not wholly determine this controversy, for the Constitution contemplates that in the end our own judgment will be brought to bear on the question of the acceptability of the death penalty under the Eighth Amendment. Nevertheless, the legislative rejection of capital punishment for rape strongly confirms our own judgment, which is that death is indeed a disproportionate penalty for the crime of raping an adult woman.

We do not discount the seriousness of rape as a crime. It is highly reprehensible, both in a moral sense and in its almost total contempt for the personal integrity and autonomy of the female victim and for the latter's privilege of choosing those with whom intimate relationships are to be established. Short of homicide, it is the "ultimate violation of self." It is also a violent crime because it normally involves force, or the threat of force or intimidation, to overcome the will and the capacity of the victim to resist. Rape is very often accompanied by physical injury to the female and can also inflict mental and psychological damage. Because it undermines the community's sense of security, there is public injury as well.

Rape is without doubt deserving of serious punishment; but in terms of moral depravity and of the injury to the person and to the public, it does not compare with murder, which does involve the unjustified taking of human life. Although it may be accompanied by another crime, rape by definition does not include the death of or even the serious injury to another person. The murderer kills; the rapist, if no more than that, does not. Life is over for the victim of the murderer; for the rape victim, life may not be nearly so happy as it was, but it is not over and normally is not beyond repair. We have the abiding conviction that the death penalty, which " is unique in its severity and irrevocability," is an excessive penalty for the rapist who, as such, does not take human life.

This does not end the matter; for under Georgia law, death may not be imposed for any capital offense, including rape, unless the jury or judge finds one of the statutory aggravating circumstances and then elects to impose that sentence. For the rapist to be executed in Georgia, it must therefore be found not only that he committed rape but also that one or more of the following aggravating circumstances were present: (1) that the rape was committed by a person with a prior record of conviction for a capital felony; (2) that the rape was committed while the offender was engaged in the commission of another capital felony, or aggravated battery; or (3) the rape "was outrageously or wantonly vile, horrible or inhuman in that it involved torture, depravity of mind, or aggravated battery to the victim." Here, the first two of these aggravating circumstances were alleged [claimed] and found by the jury.

Neither of these circumstances, nor both of them together, change our conclusion that the death sentence imposed on Coker is a disproportionate punishment for rape. Coker had prior convictions for capital felonies - rape, murder, and kidnaping - but these prior convictions do not change the fact that the instant crime being punished is a rape not involving the taking of life.

It is also true that the present rape occurred while Coker was committing armed robbery, a felony for which the Georgia statutes authorize the death penalty. But Coker was tried for the robbery offense as well as for rape and received a separate life sentence for this crime; the jury did not deem the robbery itself deserving of the death penalty, even though accompanied by the aggravating circumstance, . . . that Coker had been convicted of a prior capital crime.

We note finally that in Georgia a person commits murder when he unlawfully and with malice aforethought, either express or implied, causes the death of another human being. He also commits that crime when in the commission of a felony he causes the death of another human being, irrespective of malice. But even where the killing is deliberate, it is not punishable by death absent proof of aggravating circumstances. It is difficult to accept the notion, and we do not, that the rapist, with or without aggravating circumstances, should be punished more heavily than the deliberate killer as long as the rapist does not himself take the life of his victim. The judgment of the Georgia Supreme Court upholding the death sentence is reversed, and the case is remanded [returned] to that court for further proceedings not inconsistent with this opinion. So ordered.

[The] legislative rejection of capital punishment for rape strongly confirms our own judgment, which is that death is indeed a disproportionate penalty for the crime of raping an adult woman.

Rape is without doubt deserving of serious punishment; but in terms of moral depravity and of the injury to the person and to the public, it does not compare with murder, which does involve the unjustified taking of human life.

Mitigating Circumstances
Eddings v. Oklahoma

We are concerned here only with the manner of the imposition of the ultimate penalty: the death sentence imposed for the crime of murder upon an emotionally disturbed youth with a disturbed child's immaturity.

- Justice Lewis Powell

On April 4, 1977 Monty Lee Eddings, a sixteen-year-old runaway, driving a car erratically on the Oklahoma Turnpike, was pulled over by Oklahoma Highway Patrolman Larry Crabtree. Eddings fired a shotgun out his window, killing Patrolman Crabtree.

Although a minor at the time of the crime, Eddings was certified for trial as an adult and charged with first-degree murder, a capital offense. At trial in a Creek County, Oklahoma Court, Eddings pled *nolo contendere* [no contest] to the charge and was convicted of murder in the first degree. The trial judge held a sentencing hearing to weigh a life or death sentence based on the aggravating and mitigating circumstances.

At the sentencing hearing the trial judge refused to consider any mitigating circumstances presented by Eddings, other than his age. He ignored the testimony about his troubled upbringing by an alcoholic mother and an abusive father, and held that the one mitigating circumstance he would consider, Eddings' youth, was insufficient to outweigh "the especially heinous, atrocious and cruel" aggravating circumstances of the crime. Eddings was sentenced to death. The Oklahoma Court of Criminal Appeals upheld the death sentence.

Eddings appealed to the U.S. Supreme Court, claiming that the trial judge had violated his Eighth Amendment rights by refusing to consider, as a mitigating factor, any circumstance other than his youth that would have served as a basis for a sentence less than death.

On January 19, 1982 the 5-4 decision of the Supreme Court was announced by Associate Justice Lewis Powell.

The *Eddings* Court

Chief Justice Warren Burger
Appointed Chief Justice by President Nixon
Served 1969 - 1986

Associate Justice William Brennan
Appointed by President Eisenhower
Served 1956 - 1990

Associate Justice Byron White
Appointed by President Kennedy
Served 1962 - 1993

Associate Justice Thurgood Marshall
Appointed by President Lyndon Johnson
Served 1967 - 1991

Associate Justice Harry Blackmun
Appointed by President Nixon
Served 1970 - 1994

Associate Justice Lewis Powell
Appointed by President Nixon
Served 1971 - 1987

Associate Justice William Rehnquist
Appointed by President Nixon
Served 1991 -

Associate Justice John Paul Stevens
Appointed by President Ford
Served 1975 -

Associate Justice Sandra Day O'Connor
Appointed by President Reagan
Served 1981 -

The legal text of *Eddings v. Oklahoma* can be found in volume 455
of *United States Reports*. Our edited text follows.

EDDINGS v. OKLAHOMA
January 19, 1982

JUSTICE LEWIS POWELL: Petitioner [one who brings an appeal to the court] Monty Lee Eddings was convicted of first-degree murder and sentenced to death. Because this sentence was imposed without "the type of individualized consideration of mitigating [tending to reduce the penalty] factors . . . required by the Eighth and Fourteenth Amendments in capital cases [those in which the death penalty may be imposed]," we reverse.

On April 4, 1977, Eddings, a 16-year-old youth, and several younger companions ran away from their Missouri homes. They traveled in a car owned by Eddings' brother, and drove without destination or purpose in a southwesterly direction, eventually reaching the Oklahoma Turnpike. Eddings had in the car a shotgun and several rifles he had taken from his father. After he momentarily lost control of the car, he was signaled to pull over by Officer Crabtree of the Oklahoma Highway Patrol. Eddings did so, and when the officer approached the car, Eddings stuck a loaded shotgun out of the window and fired, killing the officer.

Because Eddings was a juvenile, the State moved to have him certified to stand trial as an adult. Finding that there was prosecutive merit to the complaint and that Eddings was not amenable to rehabilitation within the juvenile system, the trial court granted the motion. The ruling was affirmed [upheld] on appeal. Eddings was then charged with murder in the first degree, and the District Court of Creek County found him guilty upon his plea of nolo contendere [no contest].

The Oklahoma death penalty statute provides in pertinent part:

> "Upon conviction . . . of guilt of a defendant [one charged with a crime] of murder in the first degree, the court shall conduct a separate sentencing proceeding to determine whether the defendant should be sentenced to death or life imprisonment. . . . In the sentencing proceeding, evidence may be presented as to any mitigating circumstances or as to

any of the aggravating [those tending to increase the penalty] circumstances enumerated in this act."

[The statute] lists seven separate aggravating circumstances; the statute nowhere defines what is meant by "any mitigating circumstances."

At the sentencing hearing, the State alleged three of the aggravating circumstances enumerated in the statute: that the murder was especially heinous, atrocious, or cruel, that the crime was committed for the purpose of avoiding or preventing a lawful arrest, and that there was a probability that the defendant would commit criminal acts of violence that would constitute a continuing threat to society.

In mitigation, Eddings presented substantial evidence at the hearing of his troubled youth. The testimony of his supervising Juvenile Officer indicated that Eddings had been raised without proper guidance. His parents were divorced when he was 5 years old, and until he was 14 Eddings lived with his mother without rules or supervision. There is the suggestion that Eddings' mother was an alcoholic and possibly a prostitute. By the time Eddings was 14 he no longer could be controlled, and his mother sent him to live with his father. But neither could the father control the boy. Attempts to reason and talk gave way to physical punishment. The Juvenile Officer testified that Eddings was frightened and bitter, that his father overreacted and used excessive physical punishment: "Mr. Eddings found the only thing that he thought was effectful with the boy was actual punishment, or physical violence - hitting with a strap or something like this."

. . . . Testimony from other witnesses indicated that Eddings was emotionally disturbed in general and at the time of the crime, and that his mental and emotional development were at a level several years below his age. A state psychologist stated that Eddings had a sociopathic or antisocial personality and that approximately 30% of youths suffering from such a disorder grew out of it as they aged. A sociologist specializing in juvenile offenders testified that Eddings was treatable. A psychiatrist testified that Eddings could be rehabilitated by intensive therapy over a 15- to 20-year period. He testified further that Eddings "did pull the trigger, he did kill someone, but I don't even think he knew that he was doing it." The psychiatrist suggested that, if treated, Eddings would no longer pose a serious threat to society.

. . . . At the conclusion of all the evidence, the trial judge weighed the evidence of aggravating and mitigating circumstances. He found that the State had proved each of the three alleged [charged] aggravating circumstances beyond a reasonable doubt. Turning to the evidence of mitigating circumstances, the judge found that Eddings' youth was a mitigating factor of great weight:

"I have given very serious consideration to the youth of the Defendant when this particular crime was committed. Should I fail to do this, I think I would not be carrying out my duty."

But he would not consider in mitigation the circumstances of Eddings' unhappy upbringing and emotional disturbance:

"[The] Court cannot be persuaded entirely by the . . . fact that the youth was sixteen years old when this heinous crime was committed. Nor can the Court in following the law, in my opinion, consider the fact of this young man's violent background."

Finding that the only mitigating circumstance was Eddings' youth and finding further that this circumstance could not outweigh the aggravating circumstances present, the judge sentenced Eddings to death.

The trial judge found first that the crime was "heinous, atrocious, and cruel" because "designed to inflict a high degree of pain . . . in utter indifference to the rights of Patrolman Crabtree." Second, the judge found that the crime was "committed for the purpose of avoiding or preventing a lawful arrest or prosecution." The evidence was sufficient to indicate that at the time of the offense Eddings did not wish to be returned to Missouri and that in stopping the car the officer's intent was to make a lawful arrest. Finally, the trial judge found that Eddings posed a continu-

ing threat of violence to society. There was evidence that at one
point on the day of the murder, after Eddings had been taken to
the county jail, he told two officers that "if he was loose . . . he
would shoot" them all. There was also evidence that at another
time, when an officer refused to turn off the light in Eddings'
cell, Eddings became angry and threatened the officer: "Now I
have shot one of you people, and I'll get you too if you don't turn
this light out." Based on these two "spontaneous utterances," the
trial judge found a strong likelihood that Eddings would again
commit a criminal act of violence if released.

The Court of Criminal Appeals affirmed the sentence of death. It
found that each of the aggravating circumstances alleged by the
State had been present. It recited the mitigating evidence presented by Eddings in some detail, but in the end it agreed with
the trial court that only the fact of Eddings' youth was properly
considered as a mitigating circumstance:

> "[Eddings] also argues his mental state at the time of the
> murder. He stresses his family history in saying he was suf-
> fering from severe psychological and emotional disorders, and
> that the killing was in actuality an inevitable product of the
> way he was raised. There is no doubt that the petitioner has a
> personality disorder. But all the evidence tends to show that
> he knew the difference between right and wrong at the time
> he pulled the trigger, and that is the test of criminal responsi-
> bility in this State. For the same reason, the petitioner's family
> history is useful in explaining why he behaved the way he did,
> but it does not excuse his behavior."

. . . . In *Lockett v. Ohio*, Chief Justice Burger . . . stated the rule
that we apply today: "[We] conclude that the Eighth and Fourteenth Amendments require that the sentencer . . . not be precluded from considering, as a mitigating factor, any aspect of a
defendant's character or record and any of the circumstances of
the offense that the defendant proffers as a basis for a sentence
less than death."

. . . . As the Chief Justice explained, the rule in *Lockett* is the
product of a considerable history reflecting the law's effort to

develop a system of capital punishment at once consistent and principled but also humane and sensible to the uniqueness of the individual. Since the early days of the common law [law based on usage and custom], the legal system has struggled to accommodate these twin objectives. Thus, the common law began by treating all criminal homicides as capital offenses, with a mandatory sentence of death. Later it allowed exceptions, first through an exclusion for those entitled to claim benefit of clergy and then by limiting capital punishment to murders upon "malice prepensed." In this country we attempted to soften the rigor of the system of mandatory death sentences we inherited from England, first by grading murder into different degrees of which only murder of the first degree was a capital offense and then by committing use of the death penalty to the absolute discretion of the jury. By the time of our decision in *Furman v. Georgia*, the country had moved so far from a mandatory system that the imposition of capital punishment frequently had become arbitrary and capricious.

Beginning with *Furman*, the Court has attempted to provide standards for a constitutional death penalty that would serve both goals of measured, consistent application and fairness to the accused. Thus, in *Gregg v. Georgia*, the principal opinion held that the danger of an arbitrary and capricious death penalty could be met "by a carefully drafted statute that ensures that the sentencing authority is given adequate information and guidance." By its requirement that the jury find one of the aggravating circumstances listed in the death penalty statute, and by its direction to the jury to consider "any mitigating circumstances," the Georgia statute properly confined and directed the jury's attention to the circumstances of the particular crime and to "the characteristics of the person who committed the crime. . . ."

. . . . Similarly, in *Woodson v. North Carolina*, the plurality [not a majority opinion, but one where more Justices concur than not] held that mandatory death sentencing was not a permissible response to the problem of arbitrary jury discretion. As the history of capital punishment had shown, such an approach to the problem of discretion could not succeed while the Eighth Amendment required that the individual be given his due: "the fundamental respect for humanity underlying the Eighth Amendment . . . requires consideration of the character and record of the individual offender and the circumstances of the particular offense as a constitutionally indispensable part of the process of inflicting the penalty of death."

. . . . We now apply the rule in *Lockett* to the circumstances of this case. The trial judge stated that "in following the law" he could not "consider the fact of this young man's violent background." There is no dispute that by "violent background" the trial judge was referring to the mitigating evidence of Eddings' family history. From this statement it is clear that the trial judge did not evaluate the evidence in mitigation and find it wanting as a matter of fact; rather he found that as a matter of law he was unable even to consider the evidence.

The Court of Criminal Appeals took the same approach. It found that the evidence in mitigation was not relevant because it did not tend to provide a legal excuse from criminal responsibility. Thus the court conceded that Eddings had a "personality disorder," but cast this evidence aside on the basis that "he knew the difference between right and wrong . . . and that is the test of criminal responsibility." Similarly, the evidence of Eddings' family history was "useful in explaining" his behavior, but it did not "excuse" the behavior. From these statements it appears that the Court of Criminal Appeals also considered only that evidence to be mitigating which would tend to support a legal excuse from criminal liability.

We find that the limitations placed by these courts upon the mitigating evidence they would consider violated the rule in *Lockett*. Just as the State may not by statute preclude the sentencer from considering any mitigating factor, neither may the sentencer refuse to consider, as a matter of law, any relevant mitigating evidence. In this instance, it was as if the trial judge had instructed a jury to disregard the mitigating evidence Eddings proffered on his behalf. The sentencer, and the Court of Criminal Appeals on review, may determine the weight to be given relevant mitigating evidence. But they may not give it no weight by excluding such evidence from their consideration.

Nor do we doubt that the evidence Eddings offered was relevant mitigating evidence. Eddings was a youth of 16 years at the time of the murder. Evidence of a difficult family history and of emotional disturbance is typically introduced by defendants in mitigation. In some cases, such evidence properly may be given little weight. But when the defendant was 16 years old at the time of the offense there can be no doubt that evidence of a turbulent family history, of beatings by a harsh father, and of severe emotional disturbance is particularly relevant.

The trial judge recognized that youth must be considered a relevant mitigating factor. But youth is more than a chronological fact. It is a time and condition of life when a person may be most susceptible to influence and to psychological damage. Our history is replete with laws and judicial recognition that minors, especially in their earlier years, generally are less mature and responsible than adults. Particularly "during the formative years of childhood and adolescence, minors often lack the experience, perspective, and judgment" expected of adults.

Even the normal 16-year-old customarily lacks the maturity of an adult. In this case, Eddings was not a normal 16-year-old; he had been deprived of the care, concern, and paternal attention that children deserve. On the contrary, it is not disputed that he was a juvenile with serious emotional problems, and had been raised in a neglectful, sometimes even violent, family background. In addition, there was testimony that Eddings' mental and emotional development were at a level several years below his chronological age. All of this does not suggest an absence of responsibility for the crime of murder, deliberately committed in this case. Rather, it is to say that just as the chronological age of a minor is itself a relevant mitigating factor of great weight, so must the background and mental and emotional development of a youthful defendant be duly considered in sentencing.

We are not unaware of the extent to which minors engage increasingly in violent crime. Nor do we suggest an absence of legal responsibility where a crime is committed by a minor. We are concerned here only with the manner of the imposition of the ultimate penalty: the death sentence imposed for the crime of murder upon an emotionally disturbed youth with a disturbed child's immaturity.

On remand [return to the lower courts], the state courts must consider all relevant mitigating evidence and weigh it against the evidence of the aggravating circumstances. We do not weigh the evidence for them. Accordingly, the judgment is reversed to the extent that it sustains [upholds] the imposition of the death penalty, and the case is remanded for further proceedings not inconsistent with this opinion. So ordered.

Disproportionate Punishment
Enmund v. Florida

American criminal law has long considered a defendant's intention - and therefore his moral guilt - to be critical to the degree of [his] criminal culpability.   **- Justice Byron White**

On April 1, 1975 in rural Central Florida, Earl Enmund acted as the escape driver, an accessory, when, in the course of an armed robbery, his two accomplices committed the double murder of an elderly couple, Thomas and Eunice Kersey.

In the mid-1970's, Florida was not only one of the 32 capital punishment states that authorized the death penalty for first-degree murder convictions, but was also one of the 8 capital punishment states that authorized the death penalty for those convicted as accessories to first-degree murder.

Enmund, charged as an accessory to a double murder, was charged with two counts of first-degree murder, punishable upon conviction with death. A Hardee County jury found Enmund guilty on two counts of first-degree murder. At a separate sentencing hearing, the jury recommended the death penalty to the judge who, finding that the aggravating circumstances far outweighed the mitigating circumstances, sentenced Enmund to death. On appeal to the Florida Supreme Court, Enmund argued that the state law, allowing an accessory to a first-degree murder to be punished as if he had committed the murder himself was punishment out of proportion to the crime.

Enmund appealed to the U.S. Supreme Court, arguing that disproportionate punishment was a violation of the Eighth Amendment rule against cruel and unusual punishment.

On July 2, 1982 the 5-4 decision of the Supreme Court was announced by Associate Justice Byron White.

The *Enmund* Court

Chief Justice William Rehnquist
Appointed Associate Justice by President Nixon
Appointed Chief Justice by President Reagan
Served 1971 -

Associate Justice William Brennan
Appointed by President Eisenhower
Served 1956 - 1990

Associate Justice Byron White
Appointed by President Kennedy
Served 1962 - 1993

Associate Justice Thurgood Marshall
Appointed by President Lyndon Johnson
Served 1967 - 1991

Associate Justice Harry Blackmun
Appointed by President Nixon
Served 1970 - 1994

Associate Justice John Paul Stevens
Appointed by President Ford
Served 1975 -

Associate Justice Sandra Day O'Connor
Appointed by President Reagan
Served 1981 -

Associate Justice Antonin Scalia
Appointed by President Reagan
Served 1986 -

Associate Justice Anthony Kennedy
Appointed by President Reagan
Served 1988 -

The legal text of *Enmund v. Florida* can be found in volume 458 of *United States Reports*. Our edited text follows.

ENMUND v. FLORIDA
July 2, 1982

JUSTICE BYRON WHITE: . . . . On April 1, 1975, at approximately 7:45 a. m., Thomas and Eunice Kersey, aged 86 and 74, were robbed and fatally shot at their farmhouse in central Florida. The evidence showed that Sampson and Jeanette Armstrong had gone to the back door of the Kersey house and asked for water for an overheated car. When Mr. Kersey came out of the house, Sampson Armstrong grabbed him, pointed a gun at him, and told Jeanette Armstrong to take his money. Mr. Kersey cried for help, and his wife came out of the house with a gun and shot Jeanette Armstrong, wounding her. Sampson Armstrong, and perhaps Jeanette Armstrong, then shot and killed both of the Kerseys, dragged them into the kitchen, and took their money and fled.

Two witnesses testified that they drove past the Kersey house between 7:30 and 7:40 a. m. and saw a large cream- or yellow-colored car parked beside the road about 200 yards from the house and that a man was sitting in the car. Another witness testified that at approximately 6:45 a. m. he saw Ida Jean Shaw, petitioner [one who brings an appeal to court]'s common-law wife and Jeanette Armstrong's mother, driving a yellow Buick with a vinyl top which belonged to her and petitioner Earl Enmund. Enmund was a passenger in the car along with an unidentified woman. At about 8 a.m. the same witness saw the car return at a high rate of speed. Enmund was driving, Ida Jean Shaw was in the front seat, and one of the other two people in the car was lying down across the back seat.

Enmund, Sampson Armstrong, and Jeanette Armstrong were indicted [charged] for the first-degree murder and robbery of the Kerseys. Enmund and Sampson Armstrong were tried together. The prosecutor maintained in his closing argument that "Sampson Armstrong killed the old people." The judge instructed the jury that "[t]he killing of a human being while engaged in the perpetration of or in the attempt to perpetrate the offense of robbery is murder in the first degree even though there is no premeditated design or intent to kill." He went on to instruct them that,

> "[i]n order to sustain [uphold] a conviction of first degree murder while engaging in the perpetration of or in the attempted perpetration of the crime of robbery, the evidence must establish beyond a reasonable doubt that the defendant [one charged with a crime] was actually present and was actively aiding and abetting the robbery or attempted robbery, and that the unlawful killing occurred in the perpetration of or in the attempted perpetration of the robbery."

The jury found both Enmund and Sampson Armstrong guilty of two counts of first-degree murder and one count of robbery. A separate sentencing hearing was held and the jury recommended the death penalty for both defendants [those charged with a crime] under the Florida procedure whereby the jury advises the trial judge whether to impose the death penalty. The trial judge then sentenced Enmund to death on the two counts of first-degree murder. Enmund appealed, and the Florida Supreme Court remanded [returned to the lower court] for written findings as required by [Florida law]. The trial judge found four statutory aggravating circumstances [tending to add to the offense]: the capital felony [one for which the death penalty may be imposed] was committed while Enmund was engaged in or was an accomplice in the commission of an armed robbery; the capital felony was committed for pecuniary gain; it was especially heinous, atrocious, or cruel; and Enmund was previously convicted of a felony [more serious crime] involving the use or threat of violence. The court found that "none of the statutory mitigating circumstances [those tending to lessen the penalty] applied" to Enmund and that the aggravating circumstances outweighed the mitigating circumstances. Enmund was therefore sentenced to death on each of the murder counts.

The Florida Supreme Court affirmed [upheld] Enmund's conviction and sentences. It found that "[t]here was no direct evidence at trial that Earl Enmund was present at the back door of the Kersey home when the plan to rob the elderly couple led to their being murdered." However, it rejected petitioner's argument that at most he could be found guilty of second-degree murder under Florida's felony-murder rule. The court explained that the interaction of the "'felony murder rule and the law of principals combine to make a felon generally responsible for the lethal acts of his co-felon.'" Although [Enmund] could be convicted of second-degree murder only if he were an accessory before the fact rather than a principal, the Florida Supreme Court reasoned,

> "[T]he only evidence of the degree of his participation is the jury's likely inference that he was the person in the car by the side of the road near the scene of the crimes. The jury could have concluded that he was there, a few hundred feet away, waiting to help the robbers escape with the Kerseys' money. The evidence, therefore, was sufficient to find that the appellant [one who brings an appeal to court] was a principal of the second degree, constructively present aiding and abetting the commission of the crime of robbery. This conclusion supports the verdicts of murder in the first degree. . . ."

The State Supreme Court rejected two of the four statutory aggravating circumstances found by the trial court. It held that the findings that the murders were committed in the course of a robbery and that they were committed for pecuniary gain referred to the same aspect of petitioner's crime and must be treated as only one aggravating circumstance. In addition, the court held that "[t]he recited circumstance, that the murders were especially heinous, atrocious, and cruel, cannot be approved." However, because there were two aggravating circumstances and no mitigating circumstances, the death sentence was affirmed. In so doing, the court expressly rejected Enmund's submission that because the evidence did not establish that he intended to take life, the death penalty was barred by the Eighth Amendment of the United States Constitution.

We granted Enmund's petition for certiorari [request for us to hear the case], presenting the question whether death is a valid penalty under the Eighth and Fourteenth Amendments for one who neither took life, attempted to take life, nor intended to take life.

As recounted above, the Florida Supreme Court held that the record supported no more than the inference that Enmund was the person in the car by the side of the road at the time of the killings, waiting to help the robbers escape. This was enough under Florida law to make Enmund a constructive aider and abettor and hence a principal in first-degree murder upon whom the death penalty could be imposed. It was thus irrelevant to Enmund's challenge to the death sentence that he did not himself kill and was not present at the killings; also beside the point was whether he intended that the Kerseys be killed or anticipated that lethal force would or might be used if necessary to effectuate the robbery or a safe escape. We have concluded that imposition of the death penalty in these circumstances is inconsistent with the Eighth and Fourteenth Amendments.

The Cruel and Unusual Punishments Clause of the Eighth Amendment is directed, in part, "against all punishments which by their excessive length or severity are greatly disproportioned to the offenses charged." This Court most recently held a punishment excessive in relation to the crime charged in *Coker v. Georgia*. There the plurality opinion [not a majority, but one where more Justices concur than not] concluded that the imposition of the death penalty for the rape of an adult woman "is grossly disproportionate and excessive punishment for the crime of rape and is therefore forbidden by the Eighth Amendment as cruel and unusual punishment." In reaching this conclusion, it was stressed that our judgment "should be informed by objective factors to the maximum possible extent." Accordingly, the Court looked to the historical development of the punishment at issue, legislative judgments, international opinion, and the sentencing decisions juries have made before bringing its own judgment to bear on the matter. We proceed to analyze the punishment at issue in this case in a similar manner.

The *Coker* plurality observed that "[a]t no time in the last 50 years have a majority of the States authorized death as a punishment for rape." More importantly, in reenacting death penalty laws in order to satisfy the criteria established in *Furman v. Georgia*, only three States provided the death penalty for the rape of an adult woman in their revised statutes. The plurality therefore concluded that "[t]he current judgment with respect to the death penalty for rape is not wholly unanimous among state legislatures, but it obviously weighs very heavily on the side of rejecting capital punishment as a suitable penalty for raping an adult woman."

Thirty-six state and federal jurisdictions presently authorize the death penalty. Of these, only eight jurisdictions authorize imposition of the death penalty solely for participation in a robbery in which another robber takes life. Of the remaining 28 jurisdictions, in 4 felony murder is not a capital crime. Eleven States require some culpable mental state with respect to the homicide as a prerequisite to conviction of a crime for which the death penalty is authorized. Of these 11 States, 8 make knowing, intentional, purposeful, or premeditated killing an element of capital murder. Three other States require proof of a culpable mental state short of intent, such as recklessness or extreme indifference to human life, before the death penalty may be imposed. In these 11 States, therefore, the actors in a felony murder are not subject to the death penalty without proof of their mental state, proof which was not required with respect to Enmund either under the trial court's instructions or under the law announced by the Florida Supreme Court.

Four additional jurisdictions do not permit a defendant such as Enmund to be put to death. Of these, one State flatly prohibits capital punishment in cases where the defendant did not actually commit murder. Two jurisdictions preclude the death penalty in cases such as this one where the defendant "was a principal in the offense, which was committed by another, but his participation was relatively minor, although not so minor as to constitute a defense to prosecution." One other State limits the death penalty in felony murders to narrow circumstances not involved here.

Nine of the remaining States deal with the imposition of the death penalty for a vicarious felony murder in their capital sentencing statutes. In each of these States, a defendant may not be executed solely for participating in a felony in which a person was killed if the defendant did not actually cause the victim's death. For a defendant to be executed in these States, typically the statutory aggravating circumstances which are present must outweigh mitigating factors. To be sure, a vicarious felony murderer may be sentenced to death in these jurisdictions absent an intent to kill if sufficient aggravating circumstances are present. However, six of these nine States make it a statutory mitigating circumstance that the defendant was an accomplice in a capital felony committed by another person and his participation was relatively minor. By making minimal participation in a capital felony committed by another person a mitigating circumstance, these sentencing statutes reduce the likelihood that a person will be executed for vicarious felony murder. The remaining three jurisdictions exclude felony murder from their lists of aggravating circumstances that will support a death sentence. In each of these nine States, a nontriggerman guilty of felony murder cannot be sentenced to death for the felony murder absent aggravating circumstances above and beyond the felony murder itself.

Thus only a small minority of jurisdictions - eight - allow the death penalty to be imposed solely because the defendant somehow participated in a robbery in the course of which a murder was committed. Even if the nine States are included where such a defendant could be executed for an unintended felony murder if sufficient aggravating circumstances are present to outweigh mitigating circumstances - which often include the defendant's minimal participation in the murder - only about a third of American jurisdictions would ever permit a defendant who somehow participated in a robbery where a murder occurred to be sentenced to die. Moreover, of the eight States which have enacted new death penalty statutes since 1978, none authorize capital punishment in such circumstances. While the current legislative judgment with respect to imposition of the death penalty where a defendant did not take life, attempt to take it, or intend to take life is neither "wholly unanimous among state legislatures," nor as compelling as the legislative judgments considered in *Coker*, it nevertheless weighs on the side of rejecting capital punishment for the crime at issue.

Society's rejection of the death penalty for accomplice liability in felony murders is also indicated by the sentencing decisions that juries have made. As we have previously observed, "[t]he jury . . . is a significant and reliable objective index of contemporary values because it is so directly involved." The evidence is overwhelming that American juries have repudiated imposition of the death penalty for crimes such as [Enmund]'s. First, according to [Enmund], a search of all reported appellate court decisions since 1954 in cases where a defendant was executed for homicide shows that of the 362 executions, in 339 the person executed personally committed a homicidal assault. In 2 cases the person executed had another person commit the homicide for him, and in 16 cases the facts were not reported in sufficient detail to determine whether the person executed committed the homicide. The survey revealed only 6 cases out of 362 where a nontriggerman felony murderer was executed. All six executions took place in 1955. By contrast, there were 72 executions for rape in this country between 1955 and this Court's decision in *Coker v. Georgia* in 1977.

That juries have rejected the death penalty in cases such as this one where the defendant did not commit the homicide, was not present when the killing took place, and did not participate in a plot or scheme to murder is also shown by [Enmund]'s survey of the Nation's death-row population. As of October 1, 1981, there were 796 inmates under sentences of death for homicide. Of the 739 for whom sufficient data are available, only 41 did not participate in the fatal assault on the victim. Of the 40 among the 41 for whom sufficient information was available, only 16 were not physically present when the fatal assault was committed. These 16 prisoners included only 3, including [Enmund], who were sentenced to die absent a finding that they hired or solicited someone else to kill the victim or participated in a scheme designed to kill the victim. The figures for Florida are similar. Forty-five felony murderers are currently on death row. The Florida Supreme Court either found or affirmed a trial court or jury finding that the defendant intended life to be taken in 36 cases. In eight cases the courts made no finding with respect to intent, but the defendant was the triggerman in each case. In only one case - Enmund's - there was no finding of an intent to kill and the defendant was not the triggerman. The State does not challenge this analysis of the Florida cases.

The dissent criticizes these statistics on the ground that they do not reveal the percentage of homicides that were charged as felony murders or the percentage of cases where the State sought the death penalty for an accomplice guilty of felony murder. We doubt whether it is possible to gather such information, and at any rate, it would be relevant if prosecutors rarely sought the death penalty for accomplice felony murder, for it would tend to indicate that prosecutors, who represent society's interest in punishing crime, consider the death penalty excessive for accomplice felony murder. The fact remains that we are not aware of a single person convicted of felony murder over the past quarter century who did not kill or attempt to kill, and did not intend the death of the victim, who has been executed, and that only three persons in that category are presently sentenced to die. Nor can these figures be discounted by attributing to [Enmund] the argument that "death is an unconstitutional penalty absent an intent to kill," and observing that the statistics are incomplete with respect to intent. [Enmund]'s argument is that because he did not kill, attempt to kill, and he did not intend to kill, the death penalty is disproportionate as applied to him, and the statistics he cites are adequately tailored to demonstrate that juries - and perhaps prosecutors as well - consider death a disproportionate penalty for those who fall within his category.

Although the judgments of legislatures, juries, and prosecutors weigh heavily in the balance, it is for us ultimately to judge whether the Eighth Amendment permits imposition of the death penalty on one such as Enmund who aids and abets a felony in the course of which a murder is committed by others but who does not himself kill, attempt to kill, or intend that a killing take place or that lethal force will be employed. We have concluded, along with most legislatures and juries, that it does not.

We have no doubt that robbery is a serious crime deserving serious punishment. It is not, however, a crime "so grievous an affront to humanity that the only adequate response may be the penalty of death."

"[I]t does not compare with murder, which does involve the unjustified taking of human life. Although it may be accompanied by another crime, [robbery] by definition does not include the death of or even the serious injury to another person. The murderer kills; the [robber], if no more than that, does not. Life is over for the victim of the murderer; for the [robbery] victim, life . . . is not over and normally is not beyond repair."

As was said of the crime of rape in *Coker*, we have the abiding conviction that the death penalty, which is "unique in its severity and irrevocability," is an excessive penalty for the robber who, as such, does not take human life.

Here the robbers did commit murder; but they were subjected to the death penalty only because they killed as well as robbed. The question before us is not the disproportionality of death as a penalty for murder, but rather the validity of capital punishment for Enmund's own conduct. The focus must be on his culpability, not on that of those who committed the robbery and shot the victims, for we insist on "individualized consideration as a constitutional requirement in imposing the death sentence," which means that we must focus on "relevant facets of the character and record of the individual offender." Enmund himself did not kill or attempt to kill; and, as construed [interpreted] by the Florida Supreme Court, the record before us does not warrant a finding that Enmund had any intention of participating in or facilitating a murder. Yet under Florida law death was an authorized penalty because Enmund aided and abetted a robbery in the course of which murder was committed. It is fundamental that "causing harm intentionally must be punished more severely than causing the same harm unintentionally." Enmund did not kill or intend to kill and thus his culpability is plainly different from that of the robbers who killed; yet the State treated them alike and attributed to Enmund the culpability of those who killed the Kerseys. This was impermissible under the Eighth Amendment.

In *Gregg v. Georgia* the opinion announcing the judgment observed that "[t]he death penalty is said to serve two principal social purposes: retribution and deterrence of capital crimes by prospective offenders." Unless the death penalty when applied to those in Enmund's position measurably contributes to one or both of these goals, it "is nothing more than the purposeless and needless imposition of pain and suffering," and hence an unconstitutional punishment. We are quite unconvinced, however, that the threat that the death penalty will be imposed for murder will measurably deter one who does not kill and has no intention or purpose that life will be taken. Instead, it seems likely that "capital punishment can serve as a deterrent only when murder is the result of premeditation and deliberation," for if a person does not intend that life be taken or contemplate that lethal force will be employed by others, the possibility that the death penalty will be imposed for vicarious felony murder will not "enter into the cold calculus that precedes the decision to act."

It would be very different if the likelihood of a killing in the course of a robbery were so substantial that one should share the blame for the killing if he somehow participated in the felony. But competent observers have concluded that there is no basis in experience for the notion that death so frequently occurs in the course of a felony for which killing is not an essential ingredient that the death penalty should be considered as a justifiable deterrent to the felony itself. This conclusion was based on three comparisons of robbery statistics, each of which showed that only about one-half of one percent of robberies resulted in homicide. The most recent national crime statistics strongly support this conclusion. In addition to the evidence that killings only rarely occur during robberies is the fact, already noted, that however often death occurs in the course of a felony such as robbery, the death penalty is rarely imposed on one only vicariously guilty of the murder, a fact which further attenuates its possible utility as an effective deterrence.

As for retribution as a justification for executing Enmund, we think this very much depends on the degree of Enmund's culpability - what Enmund's intentions, expectations, and actions were. American criminal law has long considered a defendant's intention - and therefore his moral guilt - to be critical to "the degree of [his] criminal culpability," and the Court has found criminal penalties to be unconstitutionally excessive in the absence of intentional wrongdoing. In *Robinson v. California*, a statute making narcotics addiction a crime, even though such addiction "is apparently an illness which may be contracted innocently or involuntarily," was struck down under the Eighth Amendment. Similarly, in *Weems v. United States*, the Court invalidated a statute making it a crime for a public official to make a false entry in a public record but not requiring the offender to "injur[e] any one by his act or inten[d] to injure any one." The Court employed a similar approach in *Godfrey v. Georgia*, reversing a death sentence based on the existence of an aggravating circumstance because the defendant's crime did not reflect "a consciousness materially more 'depraved' than that of any person guilty of murder."

For purposes of imposing the death penalty, Enmund's criminal culpability must be limited to his participation in the robbery, and his punishment must be tailored to his personal responsibility and moral guilt. Putting Enmund to death to avenge two killings that he did not commit and had no intention of committing or causing does not measurably contribute to the retributive end of ensuring that the criminal gets his just deserts. This is the judgment of most of the legislatures that have recently addressed the matter, and we have no reason to disagree with that judgment for purposes of construing and applying the Eighth Amendment.

Because the Florida Supreme Court affirmed the death penalty in this case in the absence of proof that Enmund killed or attempted to kill, and regardless of whether Enmund intended or contemplated that life would be taken, we reverse the judgment upholding the death penalty and remand for further proceedings not inconsistent with this opinion. So ordered.

Executing The Insane
Ford v. Wainwright

The Eighth Amendment prohibits the State from inflicting the penalty of death upon a prisoner who is insane. **- Justice Thurgood Marshall**

Alvin Bernard Ford, convicted of first-degree murder in 1974, was on Florida's death row awaiting execution when, beginning in 1982, his mental state became increasingly confused and delusional. After extensive evaluation by two defense psychiatrists, Ford was diagnosed as suffering from a severe, uncontrollable mental illness, closely resembling paranoid schizophrenia, which, in their opinion, affected his ability to assist in his own defense. This diagnosis of a severe mental illness, if upheld under Florida law, would, under the Eighth Amendment, bar Ford's execution.

No U.S. State allowed for the execution of a person who met their legal definition of mental incompetence. Ford's defense appealed to the Governor of Florida for a condemned prisoner's competency hearing, which, if he was judged insane, would prevent his pending execution. Three State-appointed psychiatrists interviewed Ford and reported that, although he was suffered from a mental illness, he was still able to understand why the State was putting him to death. Upon reviewing their reports, the Governor signed Ford's death warrant.

Ford's defense filed a *habeus corpus* petition, demanding that Warden Wainwright be ordered to physically bring Ford to a federal court for a hearing of his incompetence claim. The U.S. District Court denied this petition and, on appeal, the U.S. Court of Appeals upheld their denial. Ford, claiming his Eighth Amendment rights were being violated, appealed to the U.S. Supreme Court.

On June 26, 1986 the 5-4 decision of the Supreme Court was announced by Associate Justice Thurgood Marshall.

The *Ford* Court

Chief Justice Warren Burger
Appointed Chief Justice by President Nixon
Served 1969 - 1986

Associate Justice William Brennan
Appointed by President Eisenhower
Served 1956 - 1990

Associate Justice Byron White
Appointed by President Kennedy
Served 1962 - 1993

Associate Justice Thurgood Marshall
Appointed by President Lyndon Johnson
Served 1967 - 1991

Associate Justice Harry Blackmun
Appointed by President Nixon
Served 1970 - 1994

Associate Justice Lewis Powell
Appointed by President Nixon
Served 1971 - 1987

Associate Justice William Rehnquist
Appointed by President Nixon
Served 1971 -

Associate Justice John Paul Stevens
Appointed by President Ford
Served 1975 -

Associate Justice Sandra Day O'Connor
Appointed by President Reagan
Served 1981 -

The legal text of *Ford v. Wainwright* can be found in volume 477
of *United States Reports*. Our edited text follows.

FORD v. WAINWRIGHT
June 26, 1986

JUSTICE THURGOOD MARSHALL: For centuries no jurisdiction [authority] has countenanced the execution of the insane,
yet this Court has never decided whether the Constitution forbids
the practice. Today we keep faith with our common-law [law
based on usage and custom] heritage in holding that it does.

Alvin Bernard Ford was convicted of murder in 1974 and sentenced to death. There is no suggestion that he was incompetent
at the time of his offense, at trial, or at sentencing. In early 1982,
however, Ford began to manifest gradual changes in behavior.
They began as an occasional peculiar idea or confused percep-
tion, but became more serious over time. After reading in the
newspaper that the Ku Klux Klan had held a rally in nearby Jack-
sonville, Florida, Ford developed an obsession focused upon the
Klan. His letters to various people reveal endless brooding about
his "Klan work," and an increasingly pervasive delusion that he
had become the target of a complex conspiracy, involving the
Klan and assorted others, designed to force him to commit suicide. He believed that the prison guards, part of the conspiracy,
had been killing people and putting the bodies in the concrete
enclosures used for beds. Later, he began to believe that his
women relatives were being tortured and sexually abused some-
where in the prison. This notion developed into a delusion that
the people who were tormenting him at the prison had taken
members of Ford's family hostage. The hostage delusion took
firm hold and expanded, until Ford was reporting that 135 of his
friends and family were being held hostage in the prison, and that
only he could help them. By "day 287" of the "hostage crisis,"
the list of hostages had expanded to include "senators, Senator
Kennedy, and many other leaders." In a letter to the Attorney
General of Florida, written in 1983, Ford appeared to assume
authority for ending the "crisis," claiming to have fired a number
of prison officials. He began to refer to himself as "Pope John
Paul, III," and reported having appointed nine new justices to the
Florida Supreme Court.

Counsel for Ford asked a psychiatrist who had examined Ford earlier, Dr. Jamal Amin, to continue seeing him and to recommend appropriate treatment. On the basis of roughly 14 months of evaluation, taped conversations between Ford and his attorneys, letters written by Ford, interviews with Ford's acquaintances, and various medical records, Dr. Amin concluded in 1983 that Ford suffered from "a severe, uncontrollable, mental disease which closely resembles 'Paranoid Schizophrenia With Suicide Potential'" - a "major mental disorder . . . severe enough to substantially affect Mr. Ford's present ability to assist in the defense of his life."

Ford subsequently refused to see Dr. Amin again, believing him to have joined the conspiracy against him, and Ford's counsel sought assistance from Dr. Harold Kaufman, who interviewed Ford in November 1983. Ford told Dr. Kaufman that "I know there is some sort of death penalty, but I'm free to go whenever I want because it would be illegal and the executioner would be executed." When asked if he would be executed, Ford replied, "I can't be executed because of the landmark case. I won. *Ford v. State* will prevent executions all over." These statements appeared amidst long streams of seemingly unrelated thoughts in rapid succession. Dr. Kaufman concluded that Ford had no understanding of why he was being executed, made no connection between the homicide of which he had been convicted and the death penalty, and indeed sincerely believed that he would not be executed because he owned the prisons and could control the Governor through mind waves. Dr. Kaufman found that there was "no reasonable possibility that Mr. Ford was dissembling, malingering or otherwise putting on a performance . . . ." The following month, in an interview with his attorneys, Ford regressed further into nearly complete incomprehensibility, speaking only in a code characterized by intermittent use of the word "one," making statements such as "Hands one, face one. Mafia one. God one, father one, Pope one. Pope one. Leader one."

Counsel for Ford invoked the procedures of Florida law governing the determination of competency of a condemned inmate. Following the procedures set forth in the statute, the Governor of Florida appointed a panel of three psychiatrists to evaluate whether . . . Ford had "the mental capacity to understand the nature of the death penalty and the reasons why it was imposed upon him." At a single meeting, the three psychiatrists together interviewed Ford for approximately 30 minutes. Each doctor then filed a separate two- or three-page report with the Governor, to whom the statute delegates the final decision. One doctor concluded that Ford suffered from "psychosis with paranoia" but had "enough cognitive functioning to understand the nature and the effects of the death penalty, and why it is to be imposed on him." Another found that, although Ford was "psychotic," he did "know fully what can happen to him." The third concluded that Ford had a "severe adaptational disorder," but did "comprehend his total situation including being sentenced to death, and all of the implications of that penalty." He believed that Ford's disorder, "although severe, seem[ed] contrived and recently learned." Thus, the interview produced three different diagnoses, but accord on the question of sanity as defined by state law.

The Governor's decision was announced on April 30, 1984, when, without explanation or statement, he signed a death warrant for Ford's execution. Ford's attorneys unsuccessfully sought a hearing in state court to determine anew Ford's competency to suffer execution. Counsel then filed a petition for habeas corpus [an order to bring an issue to the court] in the United States District Court for the Southern District of Florida. . . . The District Court denied the petition. . . . The Court of Appeals granted a certificate of probable cause [the right to bring an issue to the court] and stayed [stopped] Ford's execution, and we rejected the State's effort to vacate [annul] the stay of execution. The Court of Appeals then addressed the merits of Ford's claim and a divided panel affirmed [upheld] the District Court's denial of the writ [court order]. This Court granted Ford's petition for certiorari [agreed to hear the case] in order to resolve the important issue whether the Eighth Amendment prohibits the execution of the insane and, if so, whether the District Court should have held a hearing on petitioner's [one who brings an appeal to the court] claim.

Since this Court last had occasion to consider the infliction of the death penalty upon the insane, our interpretations of the Due

Process Clause and the Eighth Amendment have evolved substantially. In *Solesbee v. Balkcom*, a condemned prisoner claimed a
due process [fair and just rights guaranteed by law] right to a judicial determination of his sanity, yet the Court did not consider
the possible existence of a right under the Eighth Amendment,
which had not yet been applied to the States. The sole question
the Court addressed was whether Georgia's procedure for ascertaining sanity adequately effectuated that State's own policy of
sparing the insane from execution. . . . The adequacy of the procedures chosen by a State to determine sanity, therefore, will de-
pend upon an issue that this Court has never addressed: whether
the Constitution places a substantive restriction on the State's
power to take the life of an insane prisoner.

There is now little room for doubt that the Eighth Amendment's
ban on cruel and unusual punishment embraces, at a minimum,
those modes or acts of punishment that had been considered
cruel and unusual at the time that the Bill of Rights was adopted.
"Although the Framers may have intended the Eighth Amendment to go beyond the scope of its English counterpart, their use
of the language of the English Bill of Rights is convincing proof
that they intended to provide at least the same protection. . . ."

Moreover, the Eighth Amendment's proscriptions [prohibitions]
are not limited to those practices condemned by the common law
in 1789. Not bound by the sparing humanitarian concessions of
our forebears, the Amendment also recognizes the "evolving
standards of decency that mark the progress of a maturing society." In addition to considering the barbarous methods generally
outlawed in the 18th century, therefore, this Court takes into account objective evidence of contemporary values before determining whether a particular punishment comports with the fundamental human dignity that the Amendment protects.

We begin, then, with the common law. The bar against executing
a prisoner who has lost his sanity bears impressive historical cre-
dentials; the practice consistently has been branded "savage and
inhuman." Blackstone explained:

"[I]diots and lunatics are not chargeable for their own acts, if committed when under these incapacities: no, not even for treason itself. Also, if a man in his sound memory commits a capital offence [a crime which may be punished by the death penalty], and before arraignment for it, he becomes mad, he ought not to be arraigned for it: because he is not able to plead to it with that advice and caution that he ought. And if, after he has pleaded, the prisoner becomes mad, he shall not be tried: for how can he make his defence? If, after he be tried and found guilty, he loses his senses before judgment, judgment shall not be pronounced; and if, after judgment, he becomes of nonsane memory, execution shall be stayed: for peradventure, says the humanity of the English law, had the prisoner been of sound memory, he might have alleged something in stay of judgment or execution."

Sir Edward Coke had earlier expressed the same view of the common law of England: "[B]y intendment of Law the execution of the offender is for example, . . . but so it is not when a mad man is executed, but should be a miserable spectacle, both against Law, and of extream inhumanity and cruelty, and can be no example to others." Other recorders of the common law concurred [agreed].

As is often true of common-law principles, the reasons for the rule are less sure and less uniform than the rule itself. One explanation is that the execution of an insane person simply offends humanity; another, that it provides no example to others and thus contributes nothing to whatever deterrence value is intended to be served by capital punishment. Other commentators postulate religious underpinnings: that it is uncharitable to dispatch an offender "into another world, when he is not of a capacity to fit himself for it." It is also said that execution serves no purpose in these cases because madness is its own punishment. . . . More recent commentators opine that the community's quest for "retribution" - the need to offset a criminal act by a punishment of equivalent "moral quality" - is not served by execution of an insane person, which has a "lesser value" than that of the crime for which he is to be punished. Unanimity of rationale, therefore, we do not find. "But whatever the reason of the law is, it is plain the law is so." We know of virtually no authority condoning the execution of the insane at English common law.

Further indications suggest that this solid proscription was carried to America, where it was early observed that "the judge is bound" to stay the execution upon insanity of the prisoner.

This ancestral legacy has not outlived its time. Today, no State in the Union permits the execution of the insane. It is clear that the ancient and humane limitation upon the State's ability to execute its sentences has as firm a hold upon the jurisprudence [science of law] of today as it had centuries ago in England. The various reasons put forth in support of the common-law restriction have no less logical, moral, and practical force than they did when first voiced. For today, no less than before, we may seriously question the retributive value of executing a person who has no comprehension of why he has been singled out and stripped of his fundamental right to life. Similarly, the natural abhorrence civilized societies feel at killing one who has no capacity to come to grips with his own conscience or deity is still vivid today. And the intuition that such an execution simply offends humanity is evidently shared across this Nation. Faced with such widespread evidence of a restriction upon sovereign power, this Court is compelled to conclude that the Eighth Amendment prohibits a State from carrying out a sentence of death upon a prisoner who is insane. Whether its aim be to protect the condemned from fear and pain without comfort of understanding, or to protect the dignity of society itself from the barbarity of exacting mindless vengeance, the restriction finds enforcement in the Eighth Amendment.

The Eighth Amendment prohibits the State from inflicting the penalty of death upon a prisoner who is insane. [Ford]'s allegation of insanity . . . , if proved, . . . would bar his execution. The question before us is whether the District Court was under an obligation to hold an evidentiary hearing on the question of Ford's sanity. In answering that question, we bear in mind that, while the underlying social values encompassed by the Eighth Amendment are rooted in historical traditions, the manner in which our judicial system protects those values is purely a matter of contemporary law. Once a substantive right or restriction is recognized in the Constitution, therefore, its enforcement is in no way confined to the rudimentary process deemed adequate in ages past.

. . . . Although the condemned prisoner does not enjoy the same presumptions accorded a defendant [one charged with a crime] who has yet to be convicted or sentenced, he has not lost the protection of the Constitution altogether; if the Constitution renders the fact or timing of his execution contingent upon establishment of a further fact, then that fact must be determined with the high regard for truth that befits a decision affecting the life or death of a human being. Thus, the ascertainment of a prisoner's sanity as a predicate to lawful execution calls for no less stringent standards than those demanded in any other aspect of a capital proceeding. Indeed, a particularly acute need for guarding against error inheres in a determination that "in the present state of the mental sciences is at best a hazardous guess however conscientious." That need is greater still because the ultimate decision will turn on the finding of a single fact. . . . In light of these concerns, the procedures employed in [Ford]'s case do not fare well.

Florida law directs the Governor, when informed that a person under sentence of death may be insane, to stay the execution and appoint a commission of three psychiatrists to examine the prisoner. "The examination of the convicted person shall take place with all three psychiatrists present at the same time." After receiving the report of the commission, the Governor must determine whether "the convicted person has the mental capacity to understand the nature of the death penalty and the reasons why it was imposed on him." If the Governor finds that the prisoner has that capacity, then a death warrant is issued; if not, then the prisoner is committed to a mental health facility. The procedure is conducted wholly within the executive branch . . . and provides the exclusive means for determining sanity.

[Ford] received the statutory process. The Governor selected three psychiatrists, who together interviewed Ford for a total of 30 minutes, in the presence of eight other people, including Ford's counsel, the State's attorneys, and correctional officials.

The Governor's order specifically directed that the attorneys should not participate in the examination in any adversarial manner. This order was consistent with the present Governor's "publicly announced policy of excluding all advocacy on the part of the condemned from the process of determining whether a person under a sentence of death is insane."

After submission of the reports of the three examining psychiatrists, reaching conflicting diagnoses but agreeing on the ultimate issue of competency, Ford's counsel attempted to submit to the Governor some other written materials, including the reports of the two other psychiatrists who had examined Ford at greater length, one of whom had concluded that the prisoner was not competent to suffer execution. The Governor's office refused to inform counsel whether the submission would be considered. The Governor subsequently issued his decision in the form of a death warrant. . . .

The first deficiency in Florida's procedure lies in its failure to include the prisoner in the truth-seeking process. Notwithstanding this Court's longstanding pronouncement that "[t]he fundamental requisite of due process of law is the opportunity to be heard," state practice does not permit any material relevant to the ultimate decision to be submitted on behalf of the prisoner facing execution. In all other proceedings leading to the execution of an accused, we have said that the factfinder must "have before it all possible relevant information about the individual defendant whose fate it must determine." And we have forbidden States to limit the capital defendant's submission of relevant evidence in mitigation [lessening] of the sentence. It would be odd were we now to abandon our insistence upon unfettered presentation of relevant information, before the final fact antecedent to execution has been found.

Rather, consistent with the heightened concern for fairness and accuracy that has characterized our review of the process requisite to the taking of a human life, we believe that any procedure that precludes the prisoner or his counsel from presenting material relevant to his sanity or bars consideration of that material by the factfinder is necessarily inadequate. "[T]he minimum assurance that the life-and-death guess will be a truly informed guess requires respect for the basic ingredient of due process, namely, an opportunity to be allowed to substantiate a claim before it is rejected."

We recently had occasion to underscore the value to be derived from a factfinder's consideration of differing psychiatric opinions when resolving contested issues of mental state. In *Ake v. Oklahoma*, we recognized that, because "psychiatrists disagree widely and frequently on what constitutes mental illness [and] on the appropriate diagnosis to be attached to given behavior and symptoms," the factfinder must resolve differences in opinion within the psychiatric profession "on the basis of the evidence offered by each party" when a defendant's sanity is at issue in a criminal trial. The same holds true after conviction; without any adversarial assistance from the prisoner's representative - especially when the psychiatric opinion he proffers is based on much more extensive evaluation than that of the state-appointed commission - the factfinder loses the substantial benefit of potentially probative [tending to prove] information. The result is a much greater likelihood of an erroneous decision.

A related flaw in the Florida procedure is the denial of any opportunity to challenge or impeach the state-appointed psychiatrists' opinions. "[C]ross-examination . . . is beyond any doubt the greatest legal engine ever invented for the discovery of truth." Cross-examination of the psychiatrists, or perhaps a less formal equivalent, would contribute markedly to the process of seeking truth in sanity disputes by bringing to light the bases for each expert's beliefs, the precise factors underlying those beliefs, any history of error or caprice of the examiner, any personal bias with respect to the issue of capital punishment, the expert's degree of certainty about his or her own conclusions, and the precise meaning of ambiguous words used in the report. Without some questioning of the experts concerning their technical conclusions, a factfinder simply cannot be expected to evaluate the various opinions, particularly when they are themselves inconsistent. The failure of the Florida procedure to afford the prisoner's representative any opportunity to clarify or challenge the state experts' opinions or methods creates a significant possibility that the ultimate decision made in reliance on those experts will be distorted.

Perhaps the most striking defect in the [Florida] procedures . . . is the State's placement of the decision wholly within the executive branch. Under this procedure, the person who appoints the experts and ultimately decides whether the State will be able to carry out the sentence that it has long sought is the Governor, whose subordinates have been responsible for initiating every stage of the prosecution of the condemned from arrest through sentencing. The commander of the State's corps of prosecutors cannot be said to have the neutrality that is necessary for reliability in the factfinding proceeding.

Historically, delay of execution on account of insanity was not a matter of executive clemency (ex mandato regis) or judicial discretion (ex arbitrio judicis); rather, it was required by law (ex necessitate legis). Thus, history affords no better basis than does logic for placing the final determination of a fact, critical to the trigger of a constitutional limitation upon the State's power, in the hands of the State's own chief executive. In no other circumstance of which we are aware is the vindication of a constitutional right entrusted to the unreviewable discretion of an administrative tribunal.

Having identified various failings of the Florida scheme, we must conclude that the State's procedures for determining sanity are inadequate to preclude federal redetermination of the constitutional issue. We do not here suggest that only a full trial on the issue of sanity will suffice to protect the federal interests; we leave to the State the task of developing appropriate ways to enforce the constitutional restriction upon its execution of sentences. It may be that some high threshold showing on behalf of the prisoner will be found a necessary means to control the number of nonmeritorious or repetitive claims of insanity. Other legitimate pragmatic considerations may also supply the boundaries of the procedural safeguards that feasibly can be provided.

Yet the lodestar of any effort to devise a procedure must be the overriding dual imperative of providing redress for those with substantial claims and of encouraging accuracy in the factfinding determination. The stakes are high, and the "evidence" will always be imprecise. It is all the more important that the adversary presentation of relevant information be as unrestricted as possible. Also essential is that the manner of selecting and using the experts responsible for producing that "evidence" be conducive to the formation of neutral, sound, and professional judgments as to the prisoner's ability to comprehend the nature of the penalty. Fidelity to these principles is the solemn obligation of a civilized society.

Today we have explicitly recognized in our law a principle that has long resided there. It is no less abhorrent today than it has been for centuries to exact in penance the life of one whose mental illness prevents him from comprehending the reasons for the penalty or its implications. . . . Having been denied a factfinding procedure "adequate to afford a full and fair hearing" on the critical issue, [Ford] is entitled to an evidentiary hearing in the District Court . . . on the question of his competence to be executed.

The judgment of the Court of Appeals is reversed, and the case is remanded [returned to the lower court] for further proceedings consistent with this opinion. It is so ordered.

Executing Minors I
Thompson v. Oklahoma

We are not persuaded that the imposition of the death penalty for offenses committed by persons under sixteen years of age has made, or can be expected to make, any measurable contribution to the goals that capital punishment is intended to achieve.   **- Justice John Paul Stevens**

In the early-1980's, eighteen of the thirty-seven capital punishment states, including Oklahoma, had set the minimum age for the imposition of the death penalty at sixteen or above at the time of the crime.

On the night of January 23, 1983, in Grady County, Oklahoma, fifteen-year-old William Wayne Thompson participated with three adults in the brutal murder of his ex-brother-in-law, Charles Keene. Thompson, who boasted, "I shot him in the head, cut his throat, and threw him in the river," was arrested on a charge of first-degree murder.

An Oklahoma District Court certified that Thompson, although defined as a "child" under state law, was eligible to stand trial as an adult. The Oklahoma Court of Criminal Appeals upheld this decision and, on December 9, 1983, a jury convicted Thompson of murder. In the trial's penalty phase the jury, rejecting his age as a mitigating factor, found that the murder had been "especially heinous, atrocious and cruel" and sentenced Thompson to death. The Oklahoma Court of Criminal Appeals upheld the death sentence.

Thompson then appealed to the U.S. Supreme Court, arguing that the execution of a person under the age of sixteen violated the Eighth Amendment's prohibition of the infliction of cruel and unusual punishment.

On June 29, 1988 the 5-3 decision of the Supreme Court was announced by Associate Justice John Paul Stevens.

The *Thompson* Court

Chief Justice William Rehnquist
Appointed Associate Justice by President Nixon
Appointed Chief Justice by President Reagan
Served 1971 -

Associate Justice William Brennan
Appointed by President Eisenhower
Served 1956 - 1990

Associate Justice Byron White
Appointed by President Kennedy
Served 1962 - 1993

Associate Justice Thurgood Marshall
Appointed by President Lyndon Johnson
Served 1967 - 1991

Associate Justice Harry Blackmun
Appointed by President Nixon
Served 1970 - 1994

Associate Justice John Paul Stevens
Appointed by President Ford
Served 1975 -

Associate Justice Sandra Day O'Connor
Appointed by President Reagan
Served 1981 -

Associate Justice Antonin Scalia
Appointed by President Reagan
Served 1986 -

The legal text of *Thompson v. Oklahoma* can be found in volume 487 of *United States Reports*. Our edited text follows.

THOMPSON v. OKLAHOMA
June 29, 1988

JUSTICE JOHN PAUL STEVENS: Petitioner [one who brings an appeal to the court] was convicted of first-degree murder and sentenced to death. The principal question presented is whether the execution of that sentence would violate the constitutional prohibition against the infliction of "cruel and unusual punishments" because petitioner [William Wayne Thompson] was only 15 years old at the time of his offense.

Because there is no claim that the punishment would be excessive if the crime had been committed by an adult, only a brief statement of facts is necessary. In concert with three older persons, [Thompson] actively participated in the brutal murder of his former brother-in-law in the early morning hours of January 23, 1983. The evidence disclosed that the victim had been shot twice, and that his throat, chest, and abdomen had been cut. He also had multiple bruises and a broken leg. His body had been chained to a concrete block and thrown into a river where it remained for almost four weeks. Each of the four participants was tried separately and each was sentenced to death.

Because [Thompson] was a "child" as a matter of Oklahoma law, the District Attorney [sought] an order finding "that said child is competent and had the mental capacity to know and appreciate the wrongfulness of his [conduct]." After a hearing, the trial court concluded "that there are virtually no reasonable prospects for rehabilitation of William Wayne Thompson within the juvenile system and that William Wayne Thompson should be held accountable for his acts as if he were an adult and should be certified to stand trial as an adult."

At the guilt phase of [Thompson]'s trial, the prosecutor introduced three color photographs showing the condition of the victim's body when it was removed from the river. Although the Court of Criminal Appeals held that the use of two of those photographs was error, it concluded that the error was harmless because the evidence of [Thompson]'s guilt was so convincing.

However, the prosecutor had also used the photographs in his closing argument during the penalty phase. The Court of Criminal Appeals did not consider whether this display was proper.

At the penalty phase of the trial, the prosecutor asked the jury to find two aggravating circumstances [tending to add to the offense]: that the murder was especially heinous, atrocious, or cruel; and that there was a probability that the defendant [one charged with a crime] would commit criminal acts of violence that would constitute a continuing threat to society. The jury found the first, but not the second, and fixed [Thompson]'s punishment at death.

The Court of Criminal Appeals affirmed [upheld] the conviction and sentence, citing its earlier opinion in *Eddings v. State*, for the proposition that "once a minor is certified to stand trial as an adult, he may also, without violating the Constitution, be punished as an adult." We granted certiorari [agreed to hear the case] to consider whether a sentence of death is cruel and unusual punishment for a crime committed by a 15-year-old child, as well as whether photographic evidence that a state court deems erroneously admitted but harmless at the guilt phase nevertheless violates a capital [where the death penalty may be imposed] defendant's constitutional rights by virtue of its being considered at the penalty phase.

The authors of the Eighth Amendment drafted a categorical prohibition against the infliction of cruel and unusual punishments, but they made no attempt to define the contours of that category. They delegated that task to future generations of judges who have been guided by the "evolving standards of decency that mark the progress of a maturing society." In performing that task the Court has reviewed the work product [preparatory material] of state legislatures and sentencing juries, and has carefully considered the reasons why a civilized society may accept or reject the death penalty in certain types of cases. Thus, in confronting the question whether the youth of the defendant - more specifically, the fact that he was less than 16 years old at the time of his offense - is a sufficient reason for denying the State the power to sentence him to death, we first review relevant legislative enactments, then refer to jury determinations, and finally explain why these indicators of contemporary standards of decency confirm our judgment that such a young person is not capable of acting with the degree of culpability [blame] that can justify the ultimate penalty.

Justice Powell has repeatedly reminded us of the importance of "the experience of mankind, as well as the long history of our law, recognizing that there are differences which must be accommodated in determining the rights and duties of children as compared with those of adults. Examples of this distinction abound in our law. . . . [A] minor is not eligible to vote, to sit on a jury, to marry without parental consent, or to purchase alcohol or cigarettes. Like all other States, Oklahoma has developed a juvenile justice system in which most offenders under the age of 18 are not held criminally responsible. Its statutes do provide, however, that a 16- or 17-year-old charged with murder and other serious felonies shall be considered an adult. Other than the special certification procedure that was used to authorize [Thompson]'s trial in this case "as an adult," apparently there are no Oklahoma statutes, either civil or criminal, that treat a person under 16 years of age as anything but a "child."

The line between childhood and adulthood is drawn in different ways by various States. There is, however, complete or near unanimity among all 50 States and the District of Columbia in treating a person under 16 as a minor for several important purposes. In no State may a 15-year-old vote or serve on a jury. Further, in all but one State a 15-year-old may not drive without parental consent, and in all but four States a 15-year-old may not marry without parental consent. Additionally, in those States that have legislated on the subject, no one under age 16 may purchase pornographic materials (50 States), and in most States that have some form of legalized gambling, minors are not permitted to participate without parental consent (42 States). Most relevant, however, is the fact that all States have enacted legislation designating the maximum age for juvenile court jurisdiction [authority] at no less than 16. All of this legislation is consistent with the experience of mankind, as well as the long history of our law, that the normal 15-year-old is not prepared to assume the full responsibilities of an adult.

Most state legislatures have not expressly confronted the question of establishing a minimum age for imposition of the death penalty. In 14 States, capital punishment is not authorized at all, and in 19 others capital punishment is authorized but no minimum age is expressly stated in the death penalty statute. One might argue on the basis of this body of legislation that there is no chronological age at which the imposition of the death penalty is unconstitutional and that our current standards of decency would still tolerate the execution of 10-year-old children. We think it self-evident that such an argument is unacceptable; indeed, no such argument has been advanced in this case. If, therefore, we accept the premise that some offenders are simply too young to be put to death, it is reasonable to put this group of statutes to one side because they do not focus on the question of where the chronological age line should be drawn. When we confine our attention to the 18 States that have expressly established a minimum age in their death penalty statutes, we find that all of them require that the defendant have attained at least the age of 16 at the time of the capital offense.

The conclusion that it would offend civilized standards of decency to execute a person who was less than 16 years old at the time of his or her offense is consistent with the views that have been expressed by respected professional organizations, by other nations that share our Anglo-American heritage, and by the leading members of the Western European community. Thus, the American Bar Association and the American Law Institute have formally expressed their opposition to the death penalty for juveniles. Although the death penalty has not been entirely abolished in the United Kingdom or New Zealand (it has been abolished in Australia, except in the State of New South Wales, where it is available for treason and piracy), in neither of those countries may a juvenile be executed. The death penalty has been abolished in West Germany, France, Portugal, The Netherlands, and all of the Scandinavian countries, and is available only for exceptional crimes such as treason in Canada, Italy, Spain, and Switzerland. Juvenile executions are also prohibited in the Soviet Union.

The second societal factor the Court has examined in determining the acceptability of capital punishment to the American sen-

sibility is the behavior of juries. In fact, the infrequent and hap-
hazard handing out of death sentences by capital juries was a
prime factor underlying our judgment in *Furman v. Georgia*, that
the death penalty, as then administered in unguided fashion, was
unconstitutional.

While it is not known precisely how many persons have been
executed during the 20th century for crimes committed under the
age of 16, a scholar has recently compiled a table revealing this
number to be between 18 and 20. All of these occurred during
the first half of the century, with the last such execution taking
place apparently in 1948. In the following year this Court observed that this "whole country has traveled far from the period
in which the death sentence was an automatic and commonplace
result of convictions . . . ." The road we have traveled during the
past four decades - in which thousands of juries have tried murder cases - leads to the unambiguous conclusion that the imposition of the death penalty on a 15-year-old offender is now generally abhorrent to the conscience of the community.

Department of Justice statistics indicate that during the years
1982 through 1986 an average of over 16,000 persons were arrested for willful criminal homicide (murder and nonnegligent
manslaughter) each year. Of that group of 82,094 persons, 1,393
were sentenced to death. Only 5 of them, including the petitioner
in this case, were less than 16 years old at the time of the offense.
Statistics of this kind can, of course, be interpreted in different
ways, but they do suggest that these five young offenders have
received sentences that are "cruel and unusual in the same way
that being struck by lightning is cruel and unusual."

"Although the judgments of legislatures, juries, and prosecutors
weigh heavily in the balance, it is for us ultimately to judge
whether the Eighth Amendment permits imposition of the death
penalty" on one such as petitioner who committed a heinous
murder when he was only 15 years old. In making that judgment,
we first ask whether the juvenile's culpability should be measured
by the same standard as that of an adult, and then consider
whether the application of the death penalty to this class of of-

fenders "measurably contributes" to the social purposes that are served by the death penalty.

It is generally agreed "that punishment should be directly related to the personal culpability of the criminal defendant." There is also broad agreement on the proposition that adolescents as a class are less mature and responsible than adults. We stressed this difference in explaining the importance of treating the defendant's youth as a mitigating factor in capital cases:

> "But youth is more than a chronological fact. It is a time and condition of life when a person may be most susceptible to influence and to psychological damage. Our history is replete with laws and judicial recognition that minors, especially in their earlier years, generally are less mature and responsible than adults. Particularly 'during the formative years of childhood and adolescence, minors often lack the experience, perspective, and judgment' expected of adults."

To add further emphasis to the special mitigating force of youth, Justice Powell quoted the following passage from the 1978 Report of the Twentieth Century Fund Task Force on Sentencing Policy Toward Young Offenders:

> "[A]dolescents, particularly in the early and middle teen years, are more vulnerable, more impulsive, and less self-disciplined than adults. Crimes committed by youths may be just as harmful to victims as those committed by older persons, but they deserve less punishment because adolescents may have less capacity to control their conduct and to think in long-range terms than adults. Moreover, youth crime as such is not exclusively the offender's fault; offenses by the young also represent a failure of family, school, and the social system, which share responsibility for the development of America's youth."

Thus, the Court has already endorsed the proposition that less culpability should attach to a crime committed by a juvenile than to a comparable crime committed by an adult. The basis for this conclusion is too obvious to require extended explanation. Inexperience, less education, and less intelligence make the teenager less able to evaluate the consequences of his or her conduct while at the same time he or she is much more apt to be motivated by mere emotion or peer pressure than is an adult. The reasons why juveniles are not trusted with the privileges and responsibilities of an adult also explain why their irresponsible conduct is not as morally reprehensible as that of an adult.

"The death penalty is said to serve two principal social purposes: retribution and deterrence of capital crimes by prospective offenders." In *Gregg [v. Georgia]* we concluded that as "an expression of society's moral outrage at particularly offensive conduct," retribution was not "inconsistent with our respect for the dignity of men." Given the lesser culpability of the juvenile offender, the teenager's capacity for growth, and society's fiduciary obligations to its children, this conclusion is simply inapplicable to the execution of a 15-year-old offender.

For such a young offender, the deterrence rationale is equally unacceptable. The Department of Justice statistics indicate that about 98% of the arrests for willful homicide involved persons who were over 16 at the time of the offense. Thus, excluding younger persons from the class that is eligible for the death penalty will not diminish the deterrent value of capital punishment for the vast majority of potential offenders. And even with respect to those under 16 years of age, it is obvious that the potential deterrent value of the death sentence is insignificant for two reasons. The likelihood that the teenage offender has made the kind of cost-benefit analysis that attaches any weight to the possibility of execution is so remote as to be virtually nonexistent. And, even if one posits such a cold-blooded calculation by a 15-year-old, it is fanciful to believe that he would be deterred by the knowledge that a small number of persons his age have been executed during the 20th century. In short, we are not persuaded that the imposition of the death penalty for offenses committed by persons under 16 years of age has made, or can be expected to make, any measurable contribution to the goals that capital punishment is intended to achieve. It is, therefore, "nothing more than the purposeless and needless imposition of pain and suffering," and thus an unconstitutional punishment.

[Thompson]'s counsel and various amici curiae [friends of the court] have asked us to "draw a line" that would prohibit the execution of any person who was under the age of 18 at the time of the offense. Our task today, however, is to decide the case before us; we do so by concluding that the Eighth and Fourteenth Amendments prohibit the execution of a person who was under 16 years of age at the time of his or her offense.

The judgment of the Court of Criminal Appeals is vacated [annulled], and the case is remanded [returned to the lower court] with instructions to enter an appropriate order vacating [Thompson]'s death sentence. It is so ordered.

Executing Minors II
Stanford v. Kentucky

We discern neither a historical nor a modern societal consensus forbidding the imposition of capital punishment on any person who murders at sixteen or seventeen years of age. **- Justice Antonin Scalia**

In the 1988 *Thompson* decision, the Court found that the death sentence imposed on a 15-year-old murderer constituted cruel and unusual punishment. The Court was next asked to apply this standard to 17- and 16-year-old murderers.

On January 7, 1981 in Jefferson County, Kentucky, Kevin Stanford, then seventeen, shot to death a woman named Barbel Poore. Stanford, a minor, was certified by a juvenile court for trial as an adult and was charged with first-degree murder. Tried and convicted, Stanford was sentenced to death. The Kentucky Supreme Court upheld his death sentence, rejecting the argument that the execution of a minor violated the Eighth Amendment's prohibition against cruel and unusual punishment.

On July 27, 1985 in Avondale, Missouri, Heath Wilkins, then sixteen, stabbed to death a woman named Nancy Allen. Wilkins, a minor, was certified by a juvenile court for trial as an adult and was charged with first-degree murder. He pled guilty and was sentenced to death. The Missouri Supreme Court upheld his death sentence, rejecting the argument that the execution of a minor violated the Eighth Amendment's prohibition against cruel and unusual punishment.

Stanford and Wilkins appealed their death sentences to the U.S. Supreme Court, which combined their cases.

On June 26, 1989 the 5-4 decision of the Supreme Court was announced by Associate Justice Antonin Scalia.

The *Stanford* Court

Chief Justice William Rehnquist
Appointed Associate Justice by President Nixon
Appointed Chief Justice by President Reagan
Served 1971 -

Associate Justice William Brennan
Appointed by President Eisenhower
Served 1956 - 1990

Associate Justice Byron White
Appointed by President Kennedy
Served 1962 - 1993

Associate Justice Thurgood Marshall
Appointed by President Lyndon Johnson
Served 1967 - 1991

Associate Justice Harry Blackmun
Appointed by President Nixon
Served 1970 - 1994

Associate Justice John Paul Stevens
Appointed by President Ford
Served 1975 -

Associate Justice Sandra Day O'Connor
Appointed by President Reagan
Served 1981 -

Associate Justice Antonin Scalia
Appointed by President Reagan
Served 1986 -

Associate Justice Anthony Kennedy
Appointed by President Reagan
Served 1988 -

The legal text of *Stanford v. Kentucky* can be found in volume 492 of *United States Reports*. Our edited text follows.

STANFORD v. KENTUCKY
June 26, 1989

JUSTICE ANTONIN SCALIA: These two consolidated cases [those of Kevin Stanford and Heath Wilkins] require us to decide whether the imposition of capital punishment [where the death penalty may be imposed] on an individual for a crime committed at 16 or 17 years of age constitutes cruel and unusual punishment under the Eighth Amendment.

The first case . . . involves the shooting death of 20-year-old Barbel Poore in Jefferson County, Kentucky. Petitioner [one who brings an appeal to the court] Kevin Stanford committed the murder on January 7, 1981, when he was approximately 17 years and 4 months of age. Stanford and his accomplice repeatedly raped and sodomized Poore during and after their commission of a robbery at a gas station where she worked as an attendant. They then drove her to a secluded area near the station, where Stanford shot her pointblank in the face and then in the back of her head. The proceeds from the robbery were roughly 300 cartons of cigarettes, two gallons of fuel, and a small amount of cash. A corrections officer testified that [Stanford] explained the murder as follows: "[H]e said, I had to shoot her, [she] lived next door to me and she would recognize me. . . . I guess we could have tied her up or something or beat [her up] . . . and tell her if she tells, we would kill her. . . . Then after he said that he started laughing."

After Stanford's arrest, a Kentucky juvenile court conducted hearings to determine whether he should be transferred for trial as an adult under [Kentucky law, which] provided that juvenile court jurisdiction [authority] could be waived and an offender tried as an adult if he was either charged with a Class A felony [more serious crime] or capital crime, or was over 16 years of age and charged with a felony. Stressing the seriousness of [Stanford]'s offenses and the unsuccessful attempts of the juvenile system to treat him for numerous instances of past delinquency, the juvenile court found certification for trial as an adult to be in the best interest of [Stanford] and the community.

Stanford was convicted of murder, first-degree sodomy, first-degree robbery, and receiving stolen property, and was sentenced to death and 45 years in prison. The Kentucky Supreme Court affirmed [upheld] the death sentence, rejecting Stanford's "deman[d] that he has a constitutional right to treatment." Finding that the record clearly demonstrated that "there was no program or treatment appropriate for the appellant [one who brings an appeal to court] in the juvenile justice system," the court held that the juvenile court did not err in certifying [Stanford] for trial as an adult. The court also stated that [Stanford]'s "age and the possibility that he might be rehabilitated were mitigating factors [tending to reduce the penalty] appropriately left to the consideration of the jury that tried him."

The second case before us today . . . involves the stabbing death of Nancy Allen, a 26-year-old mother of two who was working behind the sales counter of the convenience store she and David Allen owned and operated in Avondale, Missouri. Petitioner Heath Wilkins committed the murder on July 27, 1985, when he was approximately 16 years and 6 months of age. The record reflects that Wilkins' plan was to rob the store and murder "whoever was behind the counter" because "a dead person can't talk." While Wilkins' accomplice, Patrick Stevens, held Allen, Wilkins stabbed her, causing her to fall to the floor. When Stevens had trouble operating the cash register, Allen spoke up to assist him, leading Wilkins to stab her three more times in her chest. Two of these wounds penetrated the victim's heart. When Allen began to beg for her life, Wilkins stabbed her four more times in the neck, opening her carotid artery. After helping themselves to liquor, cigarettes, rolling papers, and approximately $450 in cash and checks, Wilkins and Stevens left Allen to die on the floor.

Because he was roughly six months short of the age of majority for purposes of criminal prosecution, Wilkins could not automatically be tried as an adult under Missouri law. Before that could happen, the juvenile court was required to terminate juvenile court jurisdiction and certify Wilkins for trial as an adult under [the section of Missouri law] which permits individuals between 14 and 17 years of age who have committed felonies to be tried as adults. Relying on the "viciousness, force and violence" of the alleged crime, [Wilkins'] maturity, and the failure of the juvenile justice system to rehabilitate him after previous delinquent acts, the juvenile court made the necessary certification.

Wilkins was charged with first-degree murder [punishable by the death penalty], armed criminal action, and carrying a concealed weapon. After the court found him competent, [Wilkins] entered guilty pleas to all charges. A punishment hearing was held, at which both the State and [Wilkins] himself urged imposition of the death sentence. Evidence at the hearing revealed that [Wilkins] had been in and out of juvenile facilities since the age of eight for various acts of burglary, theft, and arson, had attempted to kill his mother by putting insecticide into Tylenol capsules, and had killed several animals in his neighborhood. Although psychiatric testimony indicated that Wilkins had "personality disorders," the witnesses agreed that Wilkins was aware of his actions and could distinguish right from wrong.

Determining that the death penalty was appropriate, the trial court entered the following order:

"[T]he court finds beyond reasonable doubt that the following aggravating circumstances [tending to increase the penalty] exist:

"1. The murder in the first degree was committed while the defendant [one charged with a crime] was engaged in the perpetration of the felony of robbery, and

"2. The murder in the first degree involved depravity of mind and that as a result thereof, it was outrageously or wantonly vile, horrible or inhuman."

On mandatory review of Wilkins' death sentence, the Supreme Court of Missouri affirmed, rejecting the argument that the punishment violated the Eighth Amendment.

We granted certiorari [agreed to hear] in these cases, and to decide whether the Eighth Amendment precludes the death penalty for individuals who commit crimes at 16 or 17 years of age.

The thrust of both Wilkins' and Stanford's arguments is that imposition of the death penalty on those who were juveniles when they committed their crimes falls within the Eighth Amendment's prohibition against "cruel and unusual punishments." Wilkins would have us define juveniles as individuals 16 years of age and under; Stanford would draw the line at 17.

Neither [Stanford nor Wilkins] asserts that his sentence constitutes one of "those modes or acts of punishment that had been considered cruel and unusual at the time that the Bill of Rights was adopted." Nor could they support such a contention. At that time, the common law [law based on usage and custom] set the rebuttable presumption of incapacity to commit any felony at the age of 14, and theoretically permitted capital punishment to be imposed on anyone over the age of 7. In accordance with the standards of this common-law tradition, at least 281 offenders under the age of 18 have been executed in this country, and at least 126 under the age of 17.

Thus [Stanford and Wilkins] are left to argue that their punishment is contrary to the "evolving standards of decency that mark the progress of a maturing society." They are correct in asserting that this Court has "not confined the prohibition embodied in the Eighth Amendment to 'barbarous' methods that were generally outlawed in the 18th century," but instead has interpreted the Amendment "in a flexible and dynamic manner." In determining what standards have "evolved," however, we have looked not to our own conceptions of decency, but to those of modern American society as a whole. As we have said, "Eighth Amendment judgments should not be, or appear to be, merely the subjective views of individual Justices; judgment should be informed by objective factors to the maximum possible extent." This approach is dictated both by the language of the Amendment - which proscribes [prohibits] only those punishments that are both "cruel and unusual" - and by the "deference we owe to the decisions of the state legislatures under our federal system."

"[F]irst" among the 'objective indicia that reflect the public attitude toward a given sanction'" are statutes passed by society's elected representatives. Of the 37 States whose laws permit capital punishment, 15 decline to impose it upon 16-year-old offenders and 12 decline to impose it on 17-year-old offenders. This does not establish the degree of national consensus this Court has previously thought sufficient to label a particular punishment cruel and unusual. In invalidating the death penalty for rape of an adult woman, we stressed that Georgia was the sole jurisdiction that authorized such a punishment. In striking down capital punishment for participation in a robbery in which an accomplice takes a life, we emphasized that only eight jurisdictions authorized similar punishment. In finding that the Eighth Amendment precludes execution of the insane and thus requires an adequate hearing on the issue of sanity, we relied upon (in addition to the common-law rule) the fact that "no State in the Union" permitted such punishment. And in striking down a life sentence without parole under a recidivist [repeat offender] statute, we stressed that "[i]t appears that [petitioner] was treated more severely than he would have been in any other State."

Since a majority of the States that permit capital punishment authorize it for crimes committed at age 16 or above, petitioners' cases are more analogous to *Tison v. Arizona*. . . . In *Tison*, which upheld Arizona's imposition of the death penalty for major participation in a felony with reckless indifference to human life, we noted that only 11 of those jurisdictions imposing capital punishment rejected its use in such circumstances. As we noted earlier, here the number is 15 for offenders under 17, and 12 for offenders under 18. We think the same conclusion as in *Tison* is required in these cases.

[Stanford and Wilkins] make much of the recently enacted federal statute providing capital punishment for certain drug-related offenses, but limiting that punishment to offenders 18 and over. That reliance is entirely misplaced. To begin with, the statute in question does not embody a judgment by the Federal Legislature that no murder is heinous enough to warrant the execution of such a youthful offender, but merely that the narrow class [group of things with similar characteristics] of offense it defines is not.

The congressional judgment on the broader question, if apparent at all, is to be found in the law that permits 16- and 17-year-olds (after appropriate findings) to be tried and punished as adults for all federal offenses, including those bearing a capital penalty that is not limited to 18-year-olds. Moreover, even if it were true that no federal statute permitted the execution of persons under 18, that would not remotely establish - in the face of a substantial number of state statutes to the contrary - a national consensus that such punishment is inhumane, any more than the absence of a federal lottery establishes a national consensus that lotteries are socially harmful. To be sure, the absence of a federal death penalty for 16- or 17-year-olds (if it existed) might be evidence that there is no national consensus in favor of such punishment. It is not the burden of Kentucky and Missouri, however, to establish a national consensus approving what their citizens have voted to do; rather, it is the "heavy burden" of petitioners, to establish a national consensus against it. As far as the primary and most reliable indication of consensus is concerned - the pattern of enacted laws - petitioners have failed to carry that burden.

Wilkins and Stanford argue, however, that even if the laws themselves do not establish a settled consensus, the application of the laws does. That contemporary society views capital punishment of 16- and 17-year-old offenders as inappropriate is demonstrated, they say, by the reluctance of juries to impose, and prosecutors to seek, such sentences. Petitioners are quite correct that a far smaller number of offenders under 18 than over 18 have been sentenced to death in this country. From 1982 through 1988, for example, out of 2,106 total death sentences, only 15 were imposed on individuals who were 16 or under when they committed their crimes, and only 30 on individuals who were 17 at the time of the crime. And it appears that actual executions for crimes committed under age 18 accounted for only about two percent of the total number of executions that occurred between 1642 and 1986. As Wilkins points out, the last execution of a person who committed a crime under 17 years of age occurred in 1959. These statistics, however, carry little significance. Given the undisputed fact that a far smaller percentage of capital crimes are committed by persons under 18 than over 18, the discrepancy in treatment is much less than might seem. Granted, however, that a substantial discrepancy exists, that does not establish the requisite proposition that the death sentence for offenders under 18 is categorically unacceptable to prosecutors and juries. To the contrary, it is not only possible, but overwhelmingly probable, that the very considerations which induce petitioners and their supporters to believe that death should never be imposed on offenders under 18 cause prosecutors and juries to believe that it should rarely be imposed.

This last point suggests why there is also no relevance to the laws cited by [Stanford and Wilkins] and their amici [friends of the court] which set 18 or more as the legal age for engaging in various activities, ranging from driving to drinking alcoholic beverages to voting. It is, to begin with, absurd to think that one must be mature enough to drive carefully, to drink responsibly, or to vote intelligently, in order to be mature enough to understand that murdering another human being is profoundly wrong, and to conform one's conduct to that most minimal of all civilized standards. But even if the requisite degrees of maturity were comparable, the age statutes in question would still not be relevant. They do not represent a social judgment that all persons under the designated ages are not responsible enough to drive, to drink, or to vote, but at most a judgment that the vast majority are not. These laws set the appropriate ages for the operation of a system that makes its determinations in gross, and that does not conduct individualized maturity tests for each driver, drinker, or voter. The criminal justice system, however, does provide individualized testing. In the realm of capital punishment in particular, "individualized consideration [is] a constitutional requirement," and one of the individualized mitigating factors that sentencers must be permitted to consider is the defendant's age. Twenty-nine States, including both Kentucky and Missouri, have codified this constitutional requirement in laws specifically designating the defendant's age as a mitigating factor in capital cases. Moreover, the determinations required by juvenile transfer statutes to certify a juvenile for trial as an adult ensure individualized consideration of the maturity and moral responsibility of 16- and 17-year-old offenders before they are even held to stand trial as adults. The application of this particularized system to the petitioners can be declared constitutionally inadequate only if there is a consensus, not that 17 or 18 is the age at which most persons, or even almost all persons, achieve sufficient maturity to be held fully responsible for murder; but that 17 or 18 is the age before which no one can reasonably be held fully responsible. What displays society's views on this latter point are not the ages set forth in the generalized system of driving, drinking, and voting laws cited by [Stanford and Wilkins] . . . , but the ages at which the States permit their particularized capital punishment systems to be applied.

Having failed to establish a consensus against capital punishment for 16- and 17-year-old offenders through state and federal statutes and the behavior of prosecutors and juries, petitioners seek to demonstrate it through other [means], including public opinion polls, the views of interest groups, and the positions adopted by various professional associations. We decline the invitation to rest constitutional law upon such uncertain foundations. A revised national consensus so broad, so clear, and so enduring as to justify a permanent prohibition upon all units of democratic government must appear in the operative acts (laws and the application of laws) that the people have approved.

We also reject [Stanford and Wilkins]'s argument that we should invalidate capital punishment of 16- and 17-year-old offenders on the ground that it fails to serve the legitimate goals of penology. According to petitioners, it fails to deter because juveniles, possessing less developed cognitive skills than adults, are less likely to fear death; and it fails to exact just retribution because juveniles, being less mature and responsible, are also less morally blameworthy. In support of these claims, [Stanford and Wilkins] . . . marshal an array of socio-scientific evidence concerning the psychological and emotional development of 16- and 17-year-olds.

If such evidence could conclusively establish the entire lack of deterrent effect and moral responsibility, resort to the Cruel and Unusual Punishments Clause would be unnecessary; the Equal Protection Clause of the Fourteenth Amendment would invalidate these laws for lack of rational basis. But as the adjective "socio-scientific" suggests (and insofar as evaluation of moral responsibility is concerned perhaps the adjective "ethico-scientific" would be more apt), it is not demonstrable that no 16-year-old is "adequately responsible" or significantly deterred. It is rational, even if mistaken, to think the contrary. The battle must be fought, then, on the field of the Eighth Amendment; and in that struggle socio-scientific, ethico-scientific, or even purely scientific evidence is not an available weapon. The punishment is either "cruel and unusual" (i. e., society has set its face against it) or it is not. The audience for these arguments, in other words, is not this Court but the citizenry of the United States. It is they, not we, who must be persuaded. For as we stated earlier, our job is to identify the "evolving standards of decency"; to determine, not what they should be, but what they are. We have no power under the Eighth Amendment to substitute our belief in the scientific evidence for the society's apparent skepticism. In short, we emphatically reject petitioner's suggestion that the issues in this case permit us to apply our "own informed judgment," regarding the desirability of permitting the death penalty for crimes by 16- and 17-year-olds.

. . . . When this Court cast loose from the historical moorings consisting of the original application of the Eighth Amendment, it did not embark rudderless upon a wide-open sea. Rather, it limited the Amendment's extension to those practices contrary to the "evolving standards of decency that mark the progress of a maturing society." It has never been thought that this was a shorthand reference to the preferences of a majority of this Court. By reaching a decision supported neither by constitutional text nor by the demonstrable current standards of our citizens, the dissent displays a failure to appreciate that "those institutions which the Constitution is supposed to limit" include the Court itself. To say, as the dissent says, that "it is for us ultimately to judge whether the Eighth Amendment permits imposition of the death penalty," - and to mean that as the dissent means it, i. e., that it is for us to judge, not on the basis of what we perceive the Eighth Amendment originally prohibited, or on the basis of what we perceive the society through its democratic processes now overwhelmingly disapproves, but on the basis of what we think "proportionate" and "measurably contributory to acceptable goals of punishment" - to say and mean that, is to replace judges of the law with a committee of philosopher-kings.

While the dissent is correct that several of our cases have engaged in so-called "proportionality" analysis, examining whether "there is a disproportion 'between the punishment imposed and the defendant's blameworthiness,'" and whether a punishment makes any "measurable contribution to acceptable goals of punishment," we have never invalidated a punishment on this basis alone. All of our cases condemning a punishment under this mode of analysis also found that the objective indicators of state laws or jury determinations evidenced a societal consensus against that penalty. In fact, the two methodologies blend into one another, since "proportionality" analysis itself can only be conducted on the basis of the standards set by our own society; the only alternative, once again, would be our personal preferences.

We discern neither a historical nor a modern societal consensus forbidding the imposition of capital punishment on any person who murders at 16 or 17 years of age. Accordingly, we conclude that such punishment does not offend the Eighth Amendment's prohibition against cruel and unusual punishment.

The judgments of the Supreme Court of Kentucky and the Supreme Court of Missouri are therefore affirmed.

Executing The Mentally Retarded I
Penry v. Lynaugh

We cannot conclude that the Eighth Amendment precludes the execution of any mentally retarded person convicted of a capital offense simply by virtue of his or her mental retardation alone.

- Justice Sandra Day O'Connor

On October 25, 1979 in Livingston, Texas, Johnny Paul Penry, then twenty-two, brutally beat, raped, and stabbed Pamela Carpenter. Penry, a paroled rapist, was identified by the victim before she died, and he subsequently confessed to the crime. Penry was charged with capital murder. At a pre-trial competency hearing, a defense psychologist testified that Penry, with an IQ of 54, the equivalent mental age of 6½, was mildly to moderately mentally retarded. Penry, found competent to stand trial on the murder charge, pled not guilty by reason of insanity.

Penry's insanity defense was based upon the testimony of a defense psychiatrist that Penry's mild to moderate mental retardation made him incapable of telling right from wrong. Two prosecution psychiatrists testified that, while Penry had limited mental abilities, he knew the difference between right and wrong and was, at the time of the murder, legally sane. Penry was found guilty of capital murder and, after the jury found no mitigating circumstances, was sentenced to death.

Arguing that the execution of a mentally retarded individual was cruel and unusual punishment, a violation of the Eighth Amendment, Penry appealed his death sentence to the U.S. District Court and the U.S. Court of Appeals, both of which rejected his arguments. Penry carried his final appeal to the U.S. Supreme Court, which agreed to hear his case.

On June 26, 1989 the 9-0 decision of the Supreme Court was announced by Associate Justice Sandra Day O'Connor.

The *Penry* Court

Chief Justice William Rehnquist
Appointed Associate Justice by President Nixon
Appointed Chief Justice by President Reagan
Served 1971 -

Associate Justice William Brennan
Appointed by President Eisenhower
Served 1956 - 1990

Associate Justice Byron White
Appointed by President Kennedy
Served 1962 - 1993

Associate Justice Thurgood Marshall
Appointed by President Lyndon Johnson
Served 1967 - 1991

Associate Justice Harry Blackmun
Appointed by President Nixon
Served 1970 - 1994

Associate Justice John Paul Stevens
Appointed by President Ford
Served 1975 -

Associate Justice Sandra Day O'Connor
Appointed by President Reagan
Served 1981 -

Associate Justice Antonin Scalia
Appointed by President Reagan
Served 1986 -

Associate Justice Anthony Kennedy
Appointed by President Reagan
Served 1988 -

The legal text of *Penry v. Lynaugh* can be found in volume 492 of *United States Reports*. Our edited text follows.

PENRY v. LYNAUGH
June 26, 1989

JUSTICE SANDRA DAY O'CONNOR: In this case, we must decide whether petitioner [one who brings an appeal to the court], Johnny Paul Penry, was sentenced to death in violation of the Eighth Amendment because the jury was not instructed that it could consider and give effect to his mitigating evidence [tending to lessen the penalty] in imposing its sentence. We must also decide whether the Eighth Amendment categorically prohibits Penry's execution because he is mentally retarded.

On the morning of October 25, 1979, Pamela Carpenter was brutally raped, beaten, and stabbed with a pair of scissors in her home in Livingston, Texas. She died a few hours later in the course of emergency treatment. Before she died, she described her assailant. Her description led two local sheriff's deputies to suspect Penry, who had recently been released on parole after conviction on another rape charge. Penry subsequently gave two statements confessing to the crime and was charged with capital murder [punishable by the death penalty].

At a competency hearing held before trial, a clinical psychologist, Dr. Jerome Brown, testified that Penry was mentally retarded. As a child, Penry was diagnosed as having organic brain damage, which was probably caused by trauma to the brain at birth. Penry was tested over the years as having an IQ between 50 and 63, which indicates mild to moderate retardation. Dr. Brown's own testing before the trial indicated that Penry had an IQ of 54. Dr. Brown's evaluation also revealed that Penry, who was 22 years old at the time of the crime, had the mental age of a 6-1/2-year-old, which means that "he has the ability to learn and the learning or the knowledge of the average 6-1/2-year-old kid." Penry's social maturity, or ability to function in the world, was that of a 9- or 10-year-old. Dr. Brown testified that "there's a point at which anyone with [Penry's] IQ is always incompetent, but, you know, this man is more in the borderline range."

The jury found Penry competent to stand trial. The guilt-innocence phase of the trial began on March 24, 1980. The trial court determined that Penry's confessions were voluntary, and they were introduced into evidence. At trial, Penry raised an insanity defense and presented the testimony of a psychiatrist, Dr. Jose Garcia. Dr. Garcia testified that Penry suffered from organic brain damage and moderate retardation, which resulted in poor impulse control and an inability to learn from experience. Dr. Garcia indicated that Penry's brain damage was probably caused at birth, but may have been caused by beatings and multiple injuries to the brain at an early age. In Dr. Garcia's judgment, Penry was suffering from an organic brain disorder at the time of the offense which made it impossible for him to appreciate the wrongfulness of his conduct or to conform his conduct to the law.

Penry's mother testified at trial that Penry was unable to learn in school and never finished the first grade. Penry's sister testified that their mother had frequently beaten him over the head with a belt when he was a child. Penry was also routinely locked in his room without access to a toilet for long periods of time. As a youngster, Penry was in and out of a number of state schools and hospitals, until his father removed him from state schools altogether when he was 12. Penry's aunt subsequently struggled for over a year to teach Penry how to print his name.

The State introduced the testimony of two psychiatrists to rebut the testimony of Dr. Garcia. Dr. Kenneth Vogtsberger testified that although Penry was a person of limited mental ability, he was not suffering from any mental illness or defect at the time of the crime, and that he knew the difference between right and wrong and had the potential to honor the law. In his view, Penry had characteristics consistent with an antisocial personality, including an inability to learn from experience and a tendency to be impulsive and to violate society's norms. He testified further that Penry's low IQ scores under-estimated his alertness and understanding of what went on around him.

Dr. Felix Peebles also testified for the State that Penry was legally sane at the time of the offense and had a "full-blown anti-social personality." In addition, Dr. Peebles testified that he personally diagnosed Penry as being mentally retarded in 1973 and again in 1977, and that Penry "had a very bad life generally, bringing up." In Dr. Peebles' view, Penry "had been socially and emotionally deprived and he had not learned to read and write adequately." Although they disagreed with the defense psychiatrist over the extent and cause of Penry's mental limitations, both psychiatrists for the State acknowledged that Penry was a person of extremely limited mental ability, and that he seemed unable to learn from his mistakes.

The jury rejected Penry's insanity defense and found him guilty of capital murder. The following day, at the close of the penalty hearing, the jury decided the sentence to be imposed on Penry by answering three "special issues":

> "(1) whether the conduct of the defendant [one charged with a crime] that caused the death of the deceased was committed deliberately and with the reasonable expectation that the death of the deceased or another would result;

> "(2) whether there is a probability that the defendant would commit criminal acts of violence that would constitute a continuing threat to society; and

> "(3) if raised by the evidence, whether the conduct of the defendant in killing the deceased was unreasonable in response to the provocation, if any, by the deceased."

If the jury unanimously answers "yes" to each issue submitted, the trial court must sentence the defendant to death. Otherwise, the defendant is sentenced to life imprisonment.

Defense counsel raised a number of objections to the proposed charge to the jury. With respect to the first special issue, he objected that the charge failed to define the term "deliberately." With respect to the second special issue, he objected that the charge failed to define the terms "probability," "criminal acts of violence," and "continuing threat to society." Defense counsel also objected to the charge because it failed to "authorize a discretionary grant of mercy based upon the existence of mitigating circumstances" and because it "fail[ed] to require as a condition to the assessment of the death penalty that the State show beyond a reasonable doubt that any aggravating circumstances [tending to increase the penalty] found to exist outweigh any mitigating circumstances." In addition, the charge failed to instruct the jury that it may take into consideration all of the evidence whether aggravating or mitigating in nature which was submitted in the full trial of the case. Defense counsel also objected that, in light of Penry's mental retardation, permitting the jury to assess the death penalty in this case amounted to cruel and unusual punishment prohibited by the Eighth Amendment.

These objections were overruled by the trial court. The jury was then instructed that the State bore the burden of proof on the special issues, and that before any issue could be answered "yes," all 12 jurors must be convinced by the evidence beyond a reasonable doubt that the answer to that issue should be "yes." The jurors were further instructed that in answering the three special issues, they could consider all the evidence submitted in both the guilt-innocence phase and the penalty phase of the trial. The jury charge then listed the three questions, with the names of the defendant and the deceased inserted.

The jury answered "yes" to all three special issues, and Penry was sentenced to death. The Texas Court of Criminal Appeals affirmed [upheld] his conviction and sentence. . . . [They] held that imposition of the death penalty was not prohibited by virtue of Penry's mental retardation. [We] denied certiorari [a hearing]. . . .

Penry then filed this federal habeas corpus petition [an order to bring an issue to the court] challenging his death sentence. Among other claims, Penry argued that he was sentenced in violation of the Eighth Amendment because the trial court failed to instruct the jury on how to weigh mitigating factors in answering the special issues and failed to define the term "deliberately."

Penry also argued that it was cruel and unusual punishment to execute a mentally retarded person. The District Court denied relief, and Penry appealed to the Court of Appeals for the Fifth Circuit.

The Court of Appeals affirmed the District Court's judgment. . . .

We [agreed to hear the case] to resolve two questions. First, was Penry sentenced to death in violation of the Eighth Amendment because the jury was not adequately instructed to take into consideration all of his mitigating evidence and because the terms in the Texas special issues were not defined in such a way that the jury could consider and give effect to his mitigating evidence in answering them? Second, is it cruel and unusual punishment under the Eighth Amendment to execute a mentally retarded person with Penry's reasoning ability?

. . . . As we indicated in *Teague* [*v. Lane*], "[i]n general . . . a case announces a new rule when it breaks new ground or imposes a new obligation on the States or the Federal Government." Or, "[t]o put it differently, a case announces a new rule if the result was not dictated by precedent [prior decision that establishes rules for future cases] existing at the time the defendant's conviction became final." *Teague* noted that "[i]t is admittedly often difficult to determine when a case announces a new rule." Justice Harlan recognized "the inevitable difficulties that will arise in attempting 'to determine whether a particular decision has really announced a "new" rule at all or whether it has simply applied a well-established constitutional principle to govern a case which is closely analogous to those which have been previously considered in the prior case law.'"

Penry's conviction became final on January 13, 1986, when this Court denied his petition for certiorari. . . . This Court's decisions in *Lockett v. Ohio*, and *Eddings v. Oklahoma* were rendered before his conviction became final. Under the retroactivity principles adopted in *Griffith v. Kentucky*, Penry is entitled to the benefit of those decisions. Citing *Lockett* and *Eddings*, Penry argues that he was sentenced to death in violation of the Eighth Amendment because, in light of the jury instructions given, the jury was unable to fully consider and give effect to the mitigating evidence of his mental retardation and abused background, which he offered as the basis for a sentence less than death. Penry thus seeks a rule that when such mitigating evidence is presented, Texas juries must, upon request, be given jury instructions that make it possible for them to give effect to that mitigating evidence in determining whether a defendant should be sentenced to death. We conclude . . . that the rule Penry seeks is not a "new rule" under *Teague.*

Penry does not challenge the . . . validity of the Texas death penalty statute. . . . Nor does he dispute that some types of mitigating evidence can be fully considered by the sentencer in the absence of special jury instructions. Instead, Penry argues that, on the facts of this case, the jury was unable to fully consider and give effect to the mitigating evidence of his mental retardation and abused background in answering the three special issues. In our view, the relief Penry seeks does not "impos[e] a new obligation" on the State of Texas. Rather, Penry simply asks the State to fulfill the assurance upon which *Jurek [v. Texas]* was based: namely, that the special issues would be interpreted broadly enough to permit the sentencer to consider all of the relevant mitigating evidence a defendant might present in imposing sentence.

In *Jurek*, the joint opinion of Justices Stewart, Powell, and Stevens noted that the Texas statute narrowed the circumstances in which the death penalty could be imposed to five categories of murders. Thus, although Texas had not adopted a list of statutory aggravating factors that the jury must find before imposing the death penalty, "its action in narrowing the categories of murders for which a death sentence may ever be imposed serves much the same purpose," and effectively "requires the sentencing authority to focus on the particularized nature of the crime." To provide the individualized sentencing determination required by the Eighth Amendment, however, the sentencer must be allowed to consider mitigating evidence. Indeed, as *Woodson v. North Carolina* made clear, "in capital cases the fundamental respect for humanity underlying the Eighth Amendment . . . requires consideration of the character and record of the individual offender and the circumstances of the particular offense as a constitutionally indispensable part of the process of inflicting the penalty of death."

Because the Texas death penalty statute does not explicitly mention mitigating circumstances, but rather directs the jury to answer three questions, *Jurek* reasoned that the statute's constitutionality "turns on whether the enumerated questions allow consideration of particularized mitigating factors." Although the various terms in the special questions had yet to be defined, the joint opinion concluded that the sentencing scheme satisfied the Eighth Amendment on the assurance that the Texas Court of Criminal Appeals would interpret the question concerning future dangerousness so as to allow the jury to consider whatever mitigating circumstances a defendant may be able to show, including a defendant's prior criminal record, age, and mental or emotional state.

Our decisions subsequent to *Jurek* have reaffirmed that the Eighth Amendment mandates an individualized assessment of the appropriateness of the death penalty. In *Lockett v. Ohio*, a plurality [not a majority, but one where more Justices concur than not] of this Court held that the Eighth and Fourteenth Amendments require that the sentencer "not be precluded from considering, as a mitigating factor, any aspect of a defendant's character or record and any of the circumstances of the offense that the defendant proffers as a basis for a sentence less than death." Thus, the Court held unconstitutional the Ohio death penalty statute which mandated capital punishment upon a finding of one aggravating circumstance unless one of three statutory mitigating factors were present.

. . . . In *Eddings v. Oklahoma*, a majority of the Court reaffirmed that a sentencer may not be precluded from considering, and may not refuse to consider, any relevant mitigating evidence offered by the defendant as the basis for a sentence less than death. . . .

Thus, at the time Penry's conviction became final, it was clear from *Lockett* and *Eddings* that a State could not, consistent with the Eighth and Fourteenth Amendments, prevent the sentencer from considering and giving effect to evidence relevant to the defendant's background or character or to the circumstances of the offense that mitigate against imposing the death penalty. Moreover, the . . . validity of the Texas death penalty statute had been upheld in Jurek on the basis of assurances that the special issues would be interpreted broadly enough to enable sentencing juries to consider all of the relevant mitigating evidence a defendant might present. Penry argues that those assurances were not fulfilled in his particular case because, without appropriate instructions, the jury could not fully consider and give effect to the mitigating evidence of his mental retardation and abused childhood in rendering its sentencing decision. The rule Penry seeks - that when such mitigating evidence is presented, Texas juries must, upon request, be given jury instructions that make it possible for them to give effect to that mitigating evidence in determining whether the death penalty should be imposed - is not a "new rule" under *Teague* because it is dictated by *Eddings* and *Lockett*. Moreover, in light of the assurances upon which *Jurek* was based, we conclude that the relief Penry seeks does not "impos[e] a new obligation" on the State of Texas.

Underlying *Lockett* and *Eddings* is the principle that punishment should be directly related to the personal culpability of the criminal defendant. If the sentencer is to make an individualized assessment of the appropriateness of the death penalty, "evidence about the defendant's background and character is relevant because of the belief, long held by this society, that defendants who commit criminal acts that are attributable to a disadvantaged background, or to emotional and mental problems, may be less culpable than defendants who have no such excuse." Moreover, *Eddings* makes clear that it is not enough simply to allow the defendant to present mitigating evidence to the sentencer. The sentencer must also be able to consider and give effect to that evidence in imposing sentence. Only then can we be sure that the sentencer has treated the defendant as a "uniquely individual human bein[g]" and has made a reliable determination that death is the appropriate sentence. "Thus, the sentence imposed at the penalty stage should reflect a reasoned moral response to the defendant's background, character, and crime."

Although Penry offered mitigating evidence of his mental retardation and abused childhood as the basis for a sentence of life imprisonment rather than death, the jury that sentenced him was only able to express its views on the appropriate sentence by answering three questions: Did Penry act deliberately when he murdered Pamela Carpenter? Is there a probability that he will be dangerous in the future? Did he act unreasonably in response to provocation? The jury was never instructed that it could consider the evidence offered by Penry as mitigating evidence and that it could give mitigating effect to that evidence in imposing sentence.

. . . . Penry argues that his mitigating evidence of mental retardation and childhood abuse has relevance to his moral culpability beyond the scope of the special issues, and that the jury was unable to express its "reasoned moral response" to that evidence in determining whether death was the appropriate punishment. We agree. Thus, we reject the State's contrary argument that the jury was able to consider and give effect to all of Penry's mitigating evidence in answering the special issues without any jury instructions on mitigating evidence.

The first special issue asks whether the defendant acted "deliberately and with the reasonable expectation that the death of the deceased . . . would result." Neither the Texas Legislature nor the Texas Court of Criminal Appeals have defined the term "deliberately," and the jury was not instructed on the term, so we do not know precisely what meaning the jury gave to it. Assuming, however, that the jurors in this case understood "deliberately" to mean something more than that Penry was guilty of "intentionally" committing murder, those jurors may still have been unable to give effect to Penry's mitigating evidence in answering the first special issue.

Penry's mental retardation was relevant to the question whether he was capable of acting "deliberately," but it also "had relevance to [his] moral culpability beyond the scope of the special verdict questio[n]." Personal culpability is not solely a function of a defendant's capacity to act "deliberately." A rational juror at the penalty phase of the trial could have concluded, in light of Penry's confession, that he deliberately killed Pamela Carpenter to escape detection. Because Penry was mentally retarded, however, and thus less able than a normal adult to control his impulses or to evaluate the consequences of his conduct, and because of his history of childhood abuse, that same juror could also conclude that Penry was less morally "culpable than defendants who have no such excuse," but who acted "deliberately" as that term is commonly understood.

. . . . The second special issue asks "whether there is a probability that the defendant would commit criminal acts of violence that would constitute a continuing threat to society." The mitigating evidence concerning Penry's mental retardation indicated that one effect of his retardation is his inability to learn from his mistakes. Although this evidence is relevant to the second issue, it is relevant only as an aggravating factor because it suggests a "yes" answer to the question of future dangerousness. The prosecutor argued at the penalty hearing that there was "a very strong probability, based on the history of this defendant, his previous criminal record, and the psychiatric testimony that we've had in this case, that the defendant will continue to commit acts of this nature." Even in a prison setting, the prosecutor argued, Penry could hurt doctors, nurses, librarians, or teachers who worked in the prison.

Penry's mental retardation and history of abuse is thus a two-edged sword: it may diminish his blameworthiness for his crime even as it indicates that there is a probability that he will be dangerous in the future. As Judge Reavley wrote for the Court of Appeals below:

> "What was the jury to do if it decided that Penry, because of retardation, arrested emotional development and a troubled youth, should not be executed? If anything, the evidence made it more likely, not less likely, that the jury would answer

the second question yes. It did not allow the jury to consider a major thrust of Penry's evidence as mitigating evidence."

The second special issue, therefore, did not provide a vehicle for the jury to give mitigating effect to Penry's evidence of mental retardation and childhood abuse.

The third special issue asks "whether the conduct of the defendant in killing the deceased was unreasonable in response to the provocation, if any, by the deceased." On this issue, the State argued that Penry stabbed Pamela Carpenter with a pair of scissors not in response to provocation, but "for the purpose of avoiding detection." Penry's own confession indicated that he did not stab the victim after she wounded him superficially with a scissors during a struggle, but rather killed her after her struggle had ended and she was lying helpless. Even if a juror concluded that Penry's mental retardation and arrested emotional development rendered him less culpable for his crime than a normal adult, that would not necessarily diminish the "unreasonableness" of his conduct in response to "the provocation, if any, by the deceased." Thus, a juror who believed Penry lacked the moral culpability to be sentenced to death could not express that view in answering the third special issue if she also concluded that Penry's action was not a reasonable response to provocation.

The State contends, notwithstanding the three interrogatories, that Penry was free to introduce and argue the significance of his mitigating circumstances to the jury. In fact, defense counsel did argue that if a juror believed that Penry, because of the mitigating evidence of his mental retardation and abused background, did not deserve to be put to death, the juror should vote "no" on one of the special issues even if she believed the State had proved that the answer should be "yes." Thus, Penry's counsel stressed the evidence of Penry's mental retardation and abused background, and asked the jurors, "can you be proud to be a party to putting a man to death with that affliction?" He urged the jury to answer the first special issue "no" because "it would be the just answer, and I think it would be a proper answer." As for the prediction of the prosecution psychiatrist that Penry was likely to continue to get into trouble, the defense argued:

> "That may be true. But, a boy with this mentality, with this mental affliction, even though you have found that issue against us as to insanity, I don't think that there is any question in a single one of you juror's [sic] minds that there is something definitely wrong, basically, with this boy. And I think there is not a single one of you that doesn't believe that this boy had brain damage. . . ."

In effect, defense counsel urged the jury to "[t]hink about each of those special issues and see if you don't find that we're inquiring into the mental state of the defendant in each and every one of them."

In rebuttal, the prosecution countered by stressing that the jurors had taken an oath to follow the law, and that they must follow the instructions they were given in answering the special issues:

> "You've all taken an oath to follow the law and you know what the law is. . . . In answering these questions based on the evidence and following the law, and that's all that I asked you to do, is to go out and look at the evidence. The burden of proof is on the State as it has been from the beginning, and we accept that burden. And I honestly believe that we have more than met that burden, and that's the reason that you didn't hear Mr. Newman [defense attorney] argue. He didn't pick out these issues and point out to you where the State had failed to meet this burden. He didn't point out the weaknesses in the State's case because, ladies and gentlemen, I submit to you we've met our burden. . . . [Y]our job as jurors and your duty as jurors is not to act on your emotions, but to act on the law as the Judge has given it to you, and on the evidence that you have heard in this courtroom, then answer those questions accordingly."

In light of the prosecutor's argument, and in the absence of appropriate jury instructions, a reasonable juror could well have believed that there was no vehicle for expressing the view that Penry did not deserve to be sentenced to death based upon his mitigating evidence.

The State conceded . . . in this Court that if a juror concluded that Penry acted deliberately and was likely to be dangerous in the future, but also concluded that because of his mental retardation he was not sufficiently culpable to deserve the death penalty, that juror would be unable to give effect to that mitigating evidence under the instructions given in this case. The State contends, however, that to instruct the jury that it could render a discretionary grant of mercy, or say "no" to the death penalty, based on Penry's mitigating evidence, would be to return to the sort of unbridled discretion that led to *Furman v. Georgia.* We disagree.

To be sure, *Furman* held that "in order to minimize the risk that the death penalty would be imposed on a capriciously selected group of offenders, the decision to impose it had to be guided by standards so that the sentencing authority would focus on the particularized circumstances of the crime and the defendant." But as we made clear in *Gregg,* so long as the class of murderers subject to capital punishment is narrowed, there is no constitutional infirmity in a procedure that allows a jury to recommend mercy based on the mitigating evidence introduced by a defendant. . . .

In this case, in the absence of instructions informing the jury that it could consider and give effect to the mitigating evidence of Penry's mental retardation and abused background by declining to impose the death penalty, we conclude that the jury was not provided with a vehicle for expressing its "reasoned moral response" to that evidence in rendering its sentencing decision. Our reasoning in *Lockett* and *Eddings* thus compels a remand [return to the lower court] for resentencing so that we do not "risk that the death penalty will be imposed in spite of factors which may call for a less severe penalty." "When the choice is between life and death, that risk is unacceptable and incompatible with the commands of the Eighth and Fourteenth Amendments."

Penry's second claim is that it would be cruel and unusual punishment, prohibited by the Eighth Amendment, to execute a mentally retarded person like himself with the reasoning capacity of a 7-year-old. He argues that because of their mental disabilities, mentally retarded people do not possess the level of moral culpability to justify imposing the death sentence. He also argues that there is an emerging national consensus against executing the mentally retarded. The State responds that there is insufficient evidence of a national consensus against executing the retarded, and that existing procedural safeguards adequately protect the interests of mentally retarded persons such as Penry.

. . . . If we were to hold that the Eighth Amendment prohibits the execution of mentally retarded persons such as Penry, we would be announcing a "new rule." Id., at 301. Such a rule is not dictated by precedent existing at the time Penry's conviction became final. Moreover, such a rule would "brea[k] new ground" and would impose a new obligation on the States and the Federal Government.

. . . . In our view, a new rule placing a certain class of individuals beyond the State's power to punish by death is analogous to a new rule placing certain conduct beyond the State's power to punish at all. . . . As Justice Harlan wrote: "There is little societal interest in permitting the criminal process to rest at a point where it ought properly never to repose."

. . . . The Eighth Amendment categorically prohibits the infliction of cruel and unusual punishments. At a minimum, the Eighth Amendment prohibits punishment considered cruel and unusual at the time the Bill of Rights was adopted. The prohibitions of the Eighth Amendment are not limited, however, to those practices condemned by the common law [law based on usage and custom] in 1789. The prohibition against cruel and unusual punishments also recognizes the "evolving standards of decency that mark the progress of a maturing society." In discerning those "evolving standards," we have looked to objective evidence of how our society views a particular punishment today. The clearest and most reliable objective evidence of contemporary values is the legislation enacted by the country's legislatures. We have also looked to data concerning the actions of sentencing juries.

It was well settled at common law that "idiots," together with "lunatics," were not subject to punishment for criminal acts committed under those incapacities. As Blackstone wrote:

". . . . [I]diots and lunatics are not chargeable for their own acts, if committed when under these incapacities: no, not even for treason itself. . . . [A] total idiocy, or absolute insanity, excuses from the guilt, and of course from the punishment, of any criminal action committed under such deprivation of the senses. . . ."

Idiocy was understood as "a defect of understanding from the moment of birth," in contrast to lunacy, which was "a partial derangement of the intellectual faculties, the senses returning at uncertain intervals."

There was no one definition of idiocy at common law, but the term "idiot" was generally used to describe persons who had a total lack of reason or understanding, or an inability to distinguish between good and evil. Hale wrote that a person who is deaf and mute from birth "is in presumption of law an idiot . . . because he hath no possibility to understand what is forbidden by law to be done, or under what penalties: but if it can appear, that he hath the use of understanding, . . . then he may be tried, and suffer judgment and execution."

The common law prohibition against punishing "idiots" and "lunatics" for criminal acts was the precursor of the insanity defense, which today generally includes "mental defect" as well as "mental disease" as part of the legal definition of insanity.

In its emphasis on a permanent, congenital mental deficiency, the old common law notion of "idiocy" bears some similarity to the modern definition of mental retardation. The common law prohibition against punishing "idiots" generally applied, however, to persons of such severe disability that they lacked the reasoning capacity to form criminal intent or to understand the difference between good and evil. In the 19th and early 20th centuries, the term "idiot" was used to describe the most retarded of persons, corresponding to what is called "profound" and "severe" retardation today.

The common law prohibition against punishing "idiots" for their crimes suggests that it may indeed be "cruel and unusual" punishment to execute persons who are profoundly or severely retarded and wholly lacking the capacity to appreciate the wrongfulness of their actions. Because of the protections afforded by the insanity defense today, such a person is not likely to be convicted or face the prospect of punishment. Moreover, under *Ford v. Wainwright,* someone who is "unaware of the punishment they are about to suffer and why they are to suffer it" cannot be executed.

Such a case is not before us today. Penry was found competent to stand trial. In other words, he was found to have the ability to consult with his lawyer with a reasonable degree of rational understanding, and was found to have a rational as well as factual understanding of the proceedings against him. In addition, the jury rejected his insanity defense, which reflected their conclusion that Penry knew that his conduct was wrong and was capable of conforming his conduct to the requirements of the law.

Penry argues, however, that there is objective evidence today of an emerging national consensus against execution of the mentally retarded, reflecting the "evolving standards of decency that mark the progress of a maturing society." The federal Anti-Drug Abuse Act of 1988 prohibits execution of a person who is mentally retarded. Only one State, however, currently bans execution of retarded persons who have been found guilty of a capital offense. Maryland has enacted a similar statute which will take effect on July 1, 1989.

In contrast, in *Ford v. Wainwright,* which held that the Eighth Amendment prohibits execution of the insane, considerably more evidence of a national consensus was available. No State permitted the execution of the insane, and 26 States had statutes explicitly requiring suspension of the execution of a capital defendant who became insane. Other States had adopted the common law prohibition against executing the insane. Moreover, in examining the objective evidence of contemporary standards of decency in *Thompson v. Oklahoma*, the plurality noted that 18 States expressly established a minimum age in their death penalty statutes, and all of them required that the defendant have attained at least the age of 16 at the time of the offense. In our view, the two state statutes prohibiting execution of the mentally retarded, even when added to the 14 States that have rejected capital punishment completely, do not provide sufficient evidence at present of a national consensus.

Penry does not offer any evidence of the general behavior of juries with respect to sentencing mentally retarded defendants, nor of decisions of prosecutors. He points instead to several public opinion surveys that indicate strong public opposition to execution of the retarded. For example, a poll taken in Texas found that 86% of those polled supported the death penalty, but 73% opposed its application to the mentally retarded. A Florida poll found 71% of those surveyed were opposed to the execution of mentally retarded capital defendants, while only 12% were in favor. A Georgia poll found 66% of those polled opposed to the death penalty for the retarded, 17% in favor, with 16% responding that it depends how retarded the person is. In addition, the AAMR [American Association on Mental Retardation], the country's oldest and largest organization of professionals working with the mentally retarded, opposes the execution of persons who are mentally retarded. The public sentiment expressed in these and other polls and resolutions may ultimately find expression in legislation, which is an objective indicator of contemporary values upon which we can rely. But at present, there is insufficient evidence of a national consensus against executing mentally retarded people convicted of capital offenses for us to conclude that it is categorically prohibited by the Eighth Amendment.

Relying largely on objective evidence such as the judgments of legislatures and juries, we have also considered whether application of the death penalty to particular categories of crimes or classes of offenders violates the Eighth Amendment because it "makes no measurable contribution to acceptable goals of punishment and hence is nothing more than the purposeless and needless imposition of pain and suffering" or because it is "grossly out of proportion to the severity of the crime." *Gregg* noted that "[t]he death penalty is said to serve two principal social purposes: retribution and deterrence of capital crimes by prospective offenders." "The heart of the retribution rationale is that a criminal sentence must be directly related to the personal culpability of the criminal offender."

Penry argues that execution of a mentally retarded person like himself with a reasoning capacity of approximately a 7-year-old would be cruel and unusual because it is disproportionate to his degree of personal culpability. Just as the plurality in *Thompson* reasoned that a juvenile is less culpable than an adult for the same crime, Penry argues that mentally retarded people do not have the judgment, perspective, and self-control of a person of normal intelligence. In essence, Penry argues that because of his diminished ability to control his impulses, to think in long-range terms, and to learn from his mistakes, he "is not capable of acting with the degree of culpability that can justify the ultimate penalty."

The AAMR and other groups working with the mentally retarded agree with Penry. They argue as amici [friends of the court] that all mentally retarded people, regardless of their degree of retardation, have substantial cognitive and behavioral disabilities that reduce their level of blameworthiness for a capital offense. Amici do not argue that people with mental retardation cannot be held responsible or punished for criminal acts they commit. Rather, they contend that because of "disability in the areas of cognitive impairment, moral reasoning, control of impulsivity, and the ability to understand basic relationships between cause and effect," mentally retarded people cannot act with the level of moral culpability that would justify imposition of the death sentence. Thus, in their view, execution of mentally retarded people convicted of capital offenses serves no valid retributive purpose.

It is clear that mental retardation has long been regarded as a factor that may diminish an individual's culpability for a criminal act. In its most severe forms, mental retardation may result in complete exculpation [clearing of guilt] from criminal responsibility. Moreover, virtually all of the States with death penalty statutes that list statutory mitigating factors include as a mitigating circumstance evidence that "[t]he capacity of the defendant to appreciate the criminality of his conduct or to conform his conduct to the requirements of law was substantially impaired." A number of States explicitly mention "mental defect" in connection with such a mitigating circumstance. Indeed, . . . the sentencing body must be allowed to consider mental retardation as a mitigating circumstance in making the individualized determination whether death is the appropriate punishment in a particular case.

On the record before the Court today, however, I cannot conclude that all mentally retarded people of Penry's ability - by virtue of their mental retardation alone, and apart from any individualized consideration of their personal responsibility - inevitably lack the cognitive, volitional, and moral capacity to act with the degree of culpability associated with the death penalty. Mentally retarded persons are individuals whose abilities and experiences can vary greatly. As the AAMR's standard work, *Classification in Mental Retardation*, points out:

> "The term mental retardation, as commonly used today, embraces a heterogeneous population, ranging from totally dependent to nearly independent people. Although all individuals so designated share the common attributes of low intelligence and inadequacies in adaptive behavior, there are marked variations in the degree of deficit manifested and the presence or absence of associated physical handicaps, stigmata, and psychologically disordered states."

In addition to the varying degrees of mental retardation, the consequences of a retarded person's mental impairment, including the deficits in his or her adaptive behavior, "may be ameliorated through education and habilitation." Although retarded persons generally have difficulty learning from experience, some are fully "capable of learning, working, and living in their communities." In light of the diverse capacities and life experiences of mentally retarded persons, it cannot be said on the record before us today that all mentally retarded people, by definition, can never act with the level of culpability associated with the death penalty.

Penry urges us to rely on the concept of "mental age," and to hold that execution of any person with a mental age of seven or below would constitute cruel and unusual punishment. Mental age is "calculated as the chronological age of nonretarded children whose average IQ test performance is equivalent to that of the individual with mental retardation." Such a rule should not be adopted today. First, there was no finding below by the judge or jury concerning Penry's "mental age." One of Penry's expert witnesses, Dr. Brown, testified that he estimated Penry's "mental age" to be 6-1/2. That same expert estimated that Penry's "social maturity" was that of a 9- or 10-year-old. As a more general matter, the "mental age" concept, irrespective of its intuitive appeal, is problematic in several respects. As the AAMR acknowledges, "[t]he equivalence between nonretarded children and retarded adults is, of course, imprecise." The "mental age" concept may underestimate the life experiences of retarded adults, while it may overestimate the ability of retarded adults to use logic and foresight to solve problems. The mental age concept has other limitations as well. Beyond the chronological age of 15 or 16, the mean scores on most intelligence tests cease to increase significantly with age. As a result, "[t]he average mental age of the average 20-year-old is not 20 but 15 years."

Not surprisingly, courts have long been reluctant to rely on the concept of mental age as a basis for exculpating a defendant from criminal responsibility. Moreover, reliance on mental age to measure the capabilities of a retarded person for purposes of the Eighth Amendment could have a disempowering effect if applied in other areas of the law. Thus, on that premise, a mildly mentally retarded person could be denied the opportunity to enter into contracts or to marry by virtue of the fact that he had a "mental age" of a young child. In light of the inherent problems with the mental age concept, and in the absence of better evidence of a national consensus against execution of the retarded, mental age should not be adopted as a line-drawing principle in our Eighth Amendment jurisprudence [science of law].

In sum, mental retardation is a factor that may well lessen a defendant's culpability for a capital offense. But we cannot conclude today that the Eighth Amendment precludes the execution of any mentally retarded person of Penry's ability convicted of a capital offense simply by virtue of his or her mental retardation alone. So long as sentencers can consider and give effect to mitigating evidence of mental retardation in imposing sentence, an individualized determination whether "death is the appropriate punishment" can be made in each particular case. While a national consensus against execution of the mentally retarded may someday emerge reflecting the "evolving standards of decency that mark the progress of a maturing society," there is insufficient evidence of such a consensus today.

Accordingly, the judgment below is affirmed in part and reversed in part, and the case is remanded for further proceedings consistent with this opinion. It is so ordered.

Executing The Mentally Retarded II
Atkins v. Virginia

Mentally retarded defendants face a special risk of wrongful execution.
                                        - Justice John Paul Stevens

In their 1989 *Penry* decision, the Supreme Court found that the Eighth Amendment did not categorically prohibit states from executing the mentally retarded. In that year only two states prohibited their execution. By 2002, of the thirty-eight states that allowed capital punishment, eighteen had laws to protect the mentally retarded from execution. Virginia was one of the twenty that did not.

On August 16, 1996 in Yorktown, Virginia, Daryl Renard Atkins, then eighteen, kidnapped and murdered twenty-one-year-old Eric Nesbit. Tried for and convicted of capital murder, Atkins was examined by two psychologists for the penalty phase of his trial. The defense's psychologist testified that Atkins had an IQ of 59, proof of mild mental retardation. The prosecution's psychologist testified that Atkins was of at least average intelligence. The jury sentenced Atkins to death. The Virginia Supreme Court upheld the death sentence. Atkins appealed to the U.S. Supreme Court, arguing that with twelve States rejecting the death penalty altogether and an additional eighteen States rejecting the death penalty for the mentally retarded, a new national consensus against executing the mentally retarded had developed. With 3,700 prisoners awaiting execution and an estimated 5-10% of those prisoners meeting the medical definition of mental retardation - an IQ below 70 - the U.S. Supreme Court agreed to hear Atkin's challenge to Virginia's death penalty statute.

On June 20, 2002, the 6-3 decision of the Supreme Court was announced by Associate Justice John Paul Stevens.

The *Atkins* Court

Chief Justice William Rehnquist
Appointed Associate Justice by President Nixon
Appointed Chief Justice by President Reagan
Served 1971 -

Associate Justice John Paul Stevens
Appointed by President Ford
Served 1975 -

Associate Justice Sandra Day O'Connor
Appointed by President Reagan
Served 1981 -

Associate Justice Antonin Scalia
Appointed by President Reagan
Served 1986 -

Associate Justice Anthony Kennedy
Appointed by President Reagan
Served 1988 -

Associate Justice David Souter
Appointed by President Bush
Served 1990 -

Associate Justice Clarence Thomas
Appointed by President Bush
Served 1991 -

Associate Justice Ruth Bader Ginsberg
Appointed by President Clinton
Served 1993 -

Associate Justice Stephen Breyer
Appointed by President Clinton
Served 1994 -

The legal text of *Atkins v. Virginia* can be found in volume 536 of *United States Reports*. Our edited text follows.

ATKINS v. VIRGINIA
June 20, 2002

JUSTICE JOHN PAUL STEVENS: Those mentally retarded persons who meet the law's requirements for criminal responsibility should be tried and punished when they commit crimes. Because of their disabilities in areas of reasoning, judgment, and control of their impulses, however, they do not act with the level of moral culpability [blame] that characterizes the most serious adult criminal conduct. Moreover, their impairments can jeopardize the reliability and fairness of capital proceedings [where the death penalty may be imposed] against mentally retarded defendants [one charged with a crime]. Presumably for these reasons, in the 13 years since we decided [*Penry v. Lynaugh*], the American public, legislators, scholars, and judges have deliberated over the question whether the death penalty should ever be imposed on a mentally retarded criminal. The consensus reflected in those deliberations informs our answer to the question presented by this case: whether such executions are "cruel and unusual punishments" prohibited by the Eighth Amendment to the Federal Constitution.

Petitioner [one who brings an appeal to the court], Daryl Renard Atkins, was convicted of abduction, armed robbery, and capital murder, and sentenced to death. At approximately midnight on August 16, 1996, Atkins and William Jones, armed with a semi-automatic handgun, abducted Eric Nesbitt, robbed him of the money on his person, drove him to an automated teller machine in his pickup truck where cameras recorded their withdrawal of additional cash, then took him to an isolated location where he was shot eight times and killed.

Jones and Atkins both testified in the guilt phase of Atkins' trial. Each confirmed most of the details in the other's account of the incident, with the important exception that each stated that the other had actually shot and killed Nesbitt. Jones' testimony, which was both more coherent and credible than Atkins', was obviously credited by the jury and was sufficient to establish Atkins' guilt. At the penalty phase of the trial, the State introduced victim impact evidence and proved two aggravating circumstances: future dangerousness and "vileness of the offense." To prove future dangerousness, the State relied on Atkins' prior felony convictions as well as the testimony of four victims of earlier robberies and assaults. To prove the second aggravator, the prosecution relied upon the trial record, including pictures of the deceased's body and the autopsy report.

In the penalty phase, the defense relied on one witness, Dr. Evan Nelson, a forensic psychologist who had evaluated Atkins before trial and concluded that he was "mildly mentally retarded." His conclusion was based on interviews with people who knew Atkins, a review of school and court records, and the administration of a standard intelligence test which indicated that Atkins had a full scale IQ of 59.

The jury sentenced Atkins to death, but the Virginia Supreme Court ordered a second sentencing hearing because the trial court had used a misleading verdict form. At the resentencing, Dr. Nelson again testified. The State presented an expert rebuttal witness, Dr. Stanton Samenow, who expressed the opinion that Atkins was not mentally retarded, but rather was of "average intelligence, at least," and diagnosable as having antisocial personality disorder. The jury again sentenced Atkins to death.

The Supreme Court of Virginia affirmed the imposition of the death penalty. Atkins did not argue before the Virginia Supreme Court that his sentence was disproportionate to penalties imposed for similar crimes in Virginia, but he did contend "that he is mentally retarded and thus cannot be sentenced to death." The majority of the state court rejected this contention, relying on our holding in *Penry*. The Court was "not willing to commute Atkins' sentence of death to life imprisonment merely because of his IQ score."

Justice Hassell and Justice Koontz dissented. They rejected Dr. Samenow's opinion that Atkins possesses average intelligence as "incredulous as a matter of law," and concluded that "the imposition of the sentence of death upon a criminal defendant who has the mental age of a child between the ages of 9 and 12 is excessive." In their opinion, "it is indefensible to conclude that individuals who are mentally retarded are not to some degree less culpable for their criminal acts. By definition, such individuals have substantial limitations not shared by the general population. A moral and civilized society diminishes itself if its system of justice does not afford recognition and consideration of those limitations in a meaningful way."

Because of the gravity of the concerns expressed by the dissenters, and in light of the dramatic shift in the state legislative landscape that has occurred in the past 13 years, we granted certiorari [agreed to hear the case] to revisit the issue that we first addressed in the *Penry* case.

The Eighth Amendment succinctly prohibits "excessive" sanctions. It provides: "Excessive bail shall not be required, nor excessive fines imposed, nor cruel and unusual punishments inflicted." In *Weems* v. *United States,* we held that a punishment of 12 years jailed in irons at hard and painful labor for the crime of falsifying records was excessive. We explained "that it is a precept of justice that punishment for crime should be graduated and proportioned to the offense." We have repeatedly applied this proportionality precept in later cases interpreting the Eighth Amendment. Thus, even though "imprisonment for ninety days is not, in the abstract, a punishment which is either cruel or unusual," it may not be imposed as a penalty for "the 'status' of narcotic addiction," because such a sanction would be excessive. As Justice Stewart explained in *Robinson [v. California]*, "Even one day in prison would be a cruel and unusual punishment for the 'crime' of having a common cold."

A claim that punishment is excessive is judged not by the standards that prevailed in 1685 when Lord Jeffreys presided over the "Bloody Assizes" or when the Bill of Rights was adopted, but rather by those that currently prevail. As Chief Justice Warren explained in his opinion in *Trop* v. *Dulles,*

"The basic concept underlying the Eighth Amendment is nothing less than the dignity of man. . . . The Amendment must draw its meaning from the evolving standards of decency that mark the progress of a maturing society."

Proportionality review under those evolving standards should be informed by "objective factors to the maximum possible extent." We have pinpointed that the "clearest and most reliable objective evidence of contemporary values is the legislation enacted by the country's legislatures." Relying in part on such legislative evidence, we have held that death is an impermissibly excessive punishment for the rape of an adult woman, or for a defendant who neither took life, attempted to take life, nor intended to take life. In *Coker [v. Georgia]*, we focused primarily on the then-recent legislation that had been enacted in response to our decision 10 years earlier in *Furman* v. *Georgia*, to support the conclusion that the "current judgment," though "not wholly unanimous," weighed very heavily on the side of rejecting capital punishment as a "suitable penalty for raping an adult woman." The "current legislative judgment" relevant to our decision in *Enmund [v. Florida]* was less clear than in *Coker* but "nevertheless weigh[ed] on the side of rejecting capital punishment for the crime at issue."

We also acknowledged in *Coker* that the objective evidence, though of great importance, did not "wholly determine" the controversy, "for the Constitution contemplates that in the end our own judgment will be brought to bear on the question of the acceptability of the death penalty under the Eighth Amendment." For example, in *Enmund*, we concluded by expressing our own judgment about the issue:

"For purposes of imposing the death penalty, Enmund's criminal *culpability* must be limited to his participation in the robbery, and his punishment must be tailored to his personal responsibility and moral guilt. Putting Enmund to death to avenge two killings that he did not commit and had no intention of committing or causing does not measurably contribute to the retributive end of ensuring that the criminal gets his just deserts. This is the judgment of most of *the legislatures that have recently addressed the matter, and we have no reason to disagree with that judgment* for purposes of construing [interpreting] and applying the Eighth Amendment."

Thus, in cases involving a consensus, our own judgment is "brought to bear," by asking whether there is reason to disagree with the judgment reached by the citizenry and its legislators. Guided by our approach in these cases, we shall first review the judgment of legislatures that have addressed the suitability of imposing the death penalty on the mentally retarded and then consider reasons for agreeing or disagreeing with their judgment.

The parties have not called our attention to any state legislative consideration of the suitability of imposing the death penalty on mentally retarded offenders prior to 1986. In that year, the public reaction to the execution of a mentally retarded murderer in Georgia apparently led to the enactment of the first state statute prohibiting such executions. In 1988, when Congress enacted legislation reinstating the federal death penalty, it expressly provided that a "sentence of death shall not be carried out upon a person who is mentally retarded." In 1989, Maryland enacted a similar prohibition. It was in that year that we decided *Penry*, and concluded that those two state enactments, "even when added to the 14 States that have rejected capital punishment completely, do not provide sufficient evidence at present of a national consensus."

Much has changed since then. Responding to the national attention received by the Bowden execution and our decision in *Penry*, state legislatures across the country began to address the issue. In 1990 Kentucky and Tennessee enacted statutes similar to those in Georgia and Maryland, as did New Mexico in 1991, and Arkansas, Colorado, Washington, Indiana, and Kansas in 1993 and 1994. In 1995, when New York reinstated its death penalty, it emulated the Federal Government by expressly exempting the mentally retarded. Nebraska followed suit in 1998. There appear to have been no similar enactments during the next two years, but in 2000 and 2001 six more States - South Dakota, Arizona, Connecticut, Florida, Missouri, and North Carolina - joined the procession. The Texas Legislature unanimously adopted a similar bill, and bills have passed at least one house in other States, including Virginia and Nevada.

It is not so much the number of these States that is significant, but the consistency of the direction of change. Given the well-known fact that anticrime legislation is far more popular than legislation providing protections for persons guilty of violent crime, the large number of States prohibiting the execution of mentally retarded persons (and the complete absence of States passing legislation reinstating the power to conduct such executions) provides powerful evidence that today our society views mentally retarded offenders as categorically less culpable than the average criminal. The evidence carries even greater force when it is noted that the legislatures that have addressed the issue have voted overwhelmingly in favor of the prohibition. Moreover, even in those States that allow the execution of mentally retarded offenders, the practice is uncommon. Some States, for example, New Hampshire and New Jersey, continue to authorize executions, but none have been carried out in decades. Thus there is little need to pursue legislation barring the execution of the mentally retarded in those States. And it appears that even among those States that regularly execute offenders and that have no prohibition with regard to the mentally retarded, only five have executed offenders possessing a known IQ less than 70 since we decided *Penry*. The practice, therefore, has become truly unusual, and it is fair to say that a national consensus has developed against it.

To the extent there is serious disagreement about the execution of mentally retarded offenders, it is in determining which offenders are in fact retarded. In this case, for instance, the Commonwealth of Virginia disputes that Atkins suffers from mental retardation. Not all people who claim to be mentally retarded will be so impaired as to fall within the range of mentally retarded offenders about whom there is a national consensus. As was our approach in *Ford* v. *Wainwright*, with regard to insanity, "we leave to the State[s] the task of developing appropriate ways to enforce the constitutional restriction upon its execution of sentences."

This consensus unquestionably reflects widespread judgment about the relative culpability of mentally retarded offenders, and the relationship between mental retardation and the penological purposes served by the death penalty. Additionally, it suggests that some characteristics of mental retardation undermine the strength of the procedural protections that our capital jurisprudence [science of law] steadfastly guards.

As discussed above, clinical definitions of mental retardation require not only subaverage intellectual functioning, but also significant limitations in adaptive skills such as communication, self-care, and self-direction that became manifest before age 18. Mentally retarded persons frequently know the difference between right and wrong and are competent to stand trial. Because of their impairments, however, by definition they have diminished capacities to understand and process information, to communicate, to abstract from mistakes and learn from experience, to engage in logical reasoning, to control impulses, and to understand the reactions of others. There is no evidence that they are more likely to engage in criminal conduct than others, but there is abundant evidence that they often act on impulse rather than pursuant to a premeditated plan, and that in group settings they are followers rather than leaders. Their deficiencies do not warrant an exemption from criminal sanctions, but they do diminish their personal culpability.

In light of these deficiencies, our death penalty jurisprudence provides two reasons consistent with the legislative consensus that the mentally retarded should be categorically excluded from execution. First, there is a serious question as to whether either justification that we have recognized as a basis for the death penalty applies to mentally retarded offenders. *Gregg* v. *Georgia* identified "retribution and deterrence of capital crimes by prospective offenders" as the social purposes served by the death penalty. Unless the imposition of the death penalty on a mentally retarded person "measurably contributes to one or both of these goals, it 'is nothing more than the purposeless and needless imposition of pain and suffering,' and hence an unconstitutional punishment."

With respect to retribution - the interest in seeing that the offender gets his "just deserts" - the severity of the appropriate punishment necessarily depends on the culpability of the offender. Since *Gregg*, our jurisprudence has consistently confined the imposition of the death penalty to a narrow category of the most serious crimes. For example, in *Godfrey v. Georgia*, we set aside [reversed] a death sentence because the petitioner's crimes did not reflect "a consciousness materially more 'depraved' than that of any person guilty of murder." If the culpability of the average murderer is insufficient to justify the most extreme sanction available to the State, the lesser culpability of the mentally retarded offender surely does not merit that form of retribution. Thus, pursuant to our narrowing jurisprudence, which seeks to ensure that only the most deserving of execution are put to death, an exclusion for the mentally retarded is appropriate.

With respect to deterrence - the interest in preventing capital crimes by prospective offenders - "it seems likely that 'capital punishment can serve as a deterrent only when murder is the result of premeditation and deliberation.'" Exempting the mentally retarded from that punishment will not affect the "cold calculus that precedes the decision" of other potential murderers. Indeed, that sort of calculus is at the opposite end of the spectrum from behavior of mentally retarded offenders. The theory of deterrence in capital sentencing is predicated upon the notion that the increased severity of the punishment will inhibit criminal actors from carrying out murderous conduct. Yet it is the same cognitive and behavioral impairments that make these defendants less morally culpable - for example, the diminished ability to understand and process information, to learn from experience, to engage in logical reasoning, or to control impulses - that also make it less likely that they can process the information of the possibility of execution as a penalty and, as a result, control their conduct based upon that information. Nor will exempting the mentally retarded from execution lessen the deterrent effect of the death penalty with respect to offenders who are not mentally retarded. Such individuals are unprotected by the exemption and will continue to face the threat of execution. Thus, executing the mentally retarded will not measurably further the goal of deterrence.

The reduced capacity of mentally retarded offenders provides a second justification for a categorical rule making such offenders ineligible for the death penalty. The risk "that the death penalty will be imposed in spite of factors which may call for a less severe penalty" is enhanced, not only by the possibility of false confessions, but also by the lesser ability of mentally retarded defendants to make a persuasive showing of mitigation [reduction of penalty] in the face of prosecutorial evidence of one or more aggravating factors [tending to add to the penalty]. Mentally retarded defendants may be less able to give meaningful assistance to their counsel and are typically poor witnesses, and their demeanor may create an unwarranted impression of lack of remorse for their crimes. As *Penry* demonstrated, moreover, reliance on mental retardation as a mitigating factor can be a two-edged sword that may enhance the likelihood that the aggravating factor of future dangerousness will be found by the jury. Mentally retarded defendants in the aggregate face a special risk of wrongful execution.

Our independent evaluation of the issue reveals no reason to disagree with the judgment of "the legislatures that have recently addressed the matter" and concluded that death is not a suitable punishment for a mentally retarded criminal. We are not persuaded that the execution of mentally retarded criminals will measurably advance the deterrent or the retributive purpose of the death penalty. Construing and applying the Eighth Amendment in the light of our "evolving standards of decency," we therefore conclude that such punishment is excessive and that the Constitution "places a substantive restriction on the State's power to take the life" of a mentally retarded offender.

The judgment of the Virginia Supreme Court is reversed and the case is remanded [returned to the lower court] for further proceedings not inconsistent with this opinion. It is so ordered.

BIBLIOGRAPHY

Acker, James, Robert Bohm, and Charles Lanier, Editors. *America's Experiment with Capital Punishment: Reflections on the Past, Present, and Future of the Ultimate Penal Sanction.* Durham, NC: Carolina Academic Press, 1998.

Agresto, John. *The Supreme Court and Constitutional Democracy.* Ithaca, NY: Cornell University Press, 1984.

Amnesty International. *United States of America: The Death Penalty and Juvenile Offenders.* New York, NY: Amnesty International, 1991.

Baird, Robert, and Stuart E. Rosenbaum, Editors. *Punishment and the Death Penalty: The Current Debate.* Amherst, NY: Prometheus Books, 1995.

Banner, Stuart. *The Death Penalty: An American History.* Cambridge, MA: Harvard University Press, 2002.

Bedau, Hugo Adam. *The Courts, The Constitution, and Capital Punishment.* Lexington, MA: Lexington Books, 1977.

———. *Death is Different: Studies in the Morality, Law, and Politics of Capital Punishment.* Boston, MA: Northeastern University Press, 1987.

———, Editor. *The Death Penalty in America: Current Controversies.* New York, NY: Oxford University Press, 1997.

Berger, Raoul. *Death Penalties: The Supreme Court's Obstacle Course.* Cambridge, MA: Harvard University Press, 1982.

Berns, Walter. *For Capital Punishment: Crime and the Morality of the Death Penalty.* New York, NY: Basic Books, 1979.

Bohm, Robert. *Deathquest: An Introduction to the Theory and Practice of Capital Punishment in the United States.* Cincinnati, OH: Anderson Publishing, 1999.

Bosco, Antoinette. *Choosing Mercy: A Mother of Murder Victims Pleads to End the Death Penalty.* Maryknoll, NY: Orbis Books, 2001.

Bowers, William J., Glenn L. Pierce, and John F. McDevitt. *Legal Homicide: Death as Punishment in America, 1864-1982.* Boston, MA: Northeastern University Press, 1984.

Cheever, Rev. George Barrell. *A Defence of Capital Punishment.* New York, NY: Wiley and Putnam, 1846.

Conley, Ronald W.. et al., Editors. *The Criminal Justice System and Retardation.* Baltimore, MD: Paul H. Brooks, 1992.

Cox, Archibald. *The Court and the Constitution.* New York, NY: Houghton-Mifflin, 1988.

Dicks, Shirley, Editor. *Young Blood: Juvenile Justice and the Death Penalty.* Amherst, NY: Prometheus Books, 1995.

Flanders, Stephen A. *Capital Punishment.* New York, NY: Facts on File, 1991.

Galliher, John F., Larry W. Koch, Teresa J. Guess, and David Patrick Keys. *America Without the Death Penalty: States Leading the Way.* Boston, MA: Northeastern University Press, 2002.

Gettinger, Stephen H. *Sentenced to Die: The People, The Crimes, and the Controversy.* New York, NY: Macmillan, 1979.

Ginger, Ann Fagan. *The Law, The Supreme Court, and The People's Rights.* Woodbury, NY: Barron's Educational Series, 1973.

Goode, Stephen. *The Controversial Court: Supreme Court Influences on American Life.* New York, NY: Messner, 1982.

Goldman, Raphael. *Capital Punishment.* Washington, DC: CQ Press, 2002.

Gottfried, Ted. *Capital Punishment: The Death Penalty Debate.*
Berkeley Heights, NJ: Enslow Publishers, Inc., 1997.

Grabowski, John F. *The Death Penalty.* San Diego, CA: Lucent
Books, 1999.

Grossman, Mark, and Mike Dixon-Kennedy. *Encyclopedia of
Capital Punishment.* Santa Barbara, CA: ABC-CLIO, 1998.

Hale, Robert L. *A Review of Juvenile Executions in America.*
Lewiston, NY: The Edwin Mellen Press, 1997.

Harr, J. Scott, and Karen M. Hess. *Constitutional Law and the
Criminal Justice System.* Florence, KY: Wadsworth Publishing Co.,
2001.

Henderson, Harry, and Stephen A. Flanders. *Capital Punishment.*
New York, NY: Facts on File, 2000.

Kronenwetter, Michael. *Capital Punishment: A Reference Handbook.*
Santa Barbara, CA: ABC-CLIO, 2001.

Landau, Elaine. *Teens and the Death Penalty.* Hillside, NJ: Enslow
Publishers, 1992.

Latzer, Barry. *Death Penalty Cases: Leading U.S. Supreme Court Cases
on Capital Punishment.* Boston, MA: Butterworth-Heinemann,
1998.

Lifton, Robert Jay, and Greg Mitchell. *Who Owns Death? Capital
Punishment, the American Conscience, and the End of Executions.* New
York, NY: Harper-Perennial, 2002.

McFeely, William S. *Proximity to Death.* New York, NY: W.W.
Norton, 2000.

Meltsner, Michael. *Cruel and Unusual: The Supreme Court and Capital
Punishment.* New York, NY: Random House, 1973.

Miller, Kent S., and Michael L. Radelet. *Executing the Mentally Ill: The Criminal Justice System and the Case of Alvin Ford.* Thousand Oaks, CA: Sage Publications, 1993.

Mitchell, Hayley R., Editor. *The Complete History of the Death Penalty.* San Diego, CA: Greenhaven Press, 2001.

———. *The Death Penalty.* San Diego, CA: Greenhaven Press, 2000.

Nathanson, Stephen. *An Eye for an Eye?: The Morality of Punishing by Death.* Totowa, NJ: Rowman & Littlefield, 1987.

Nelson, Lane, and Burk Foster. *Death Watch: A Death Penalty Anthology.* Upper Saddle River, NJ: Prentice Hall, 2000.

Palmer, Louis J., Jr. *Encyclopedia of Capital Punishment in the United States.* Jefferson, NC: McFarland & Company, 2001.

Paternoster, Raymond. *Capital Punishment in America.* New York, NY: Lexington Books, 1991.

Pojman, Louis P., and Jeffrey Reiman. *The Death Penalty.* Lanham, MD: Rowman & Littlefield Publishing, 1998.

Prejean, Helen. *Dead Man Walking: An Eyewitness Account of the Death Penalty in the United States.* New York, NY: Vintage Books, 1994.

Radelet, Michael L., and Vandiver, Margaret. *Capital Punishment in America: An Annotated Bibliography.* New York, NY: Garland Publishing, New York, 1988.

Reed, Emily F. *The Penry Penalty: Capital Punishment and Offenders with Mental Retardation.* Lanham, MD: University Press of America, 1993.

hnquist, William H. *The Supreme Court: How It Was, How It Is.* York, NY: Morrow, 1987.

Rein, Mei Ling, Editor. *Capital Punishment: Cruel and Unusual.* Dallas, TX: Information Plus, 2002.

Sarat, Austin, Editor. *The Killing State: Capital Punishment in Law, Politics, and Culture.* New York, NY: Oxford University Press, 2001.

_____. *When the State Kills: Capital Punishment and the American Condition.* Princeton, NJ: Princeton University Press, 2001.

Schonebaum, Stephen E., Editor. *Does Capital Punishment Deter Crime?* San Diego, CA: Greenhaven Press, 1998.

Siegel, Mark A., Carol D. Foster, and Nancy R. Jacobs, Editors. *Capital Punishment: Cruel and Unusual?* Plano, TX: Information Aids, 1988.

Simon, Seymour. *Clarence Darrow on Capital Punishment.* Evanston, IL: Chicago Historical Bookworks Publishers, 1991.

Steffans, Bradley, et al. *Furman v. Georgia: Fairness and the Death Penalty.* San Diego, CA: Lucent Books, 2001.

Stewart, Gail, Editor. *The Death Penalty.* San Diego, CA: Greenhaven Press, 1997.

Streib, Victor L., Editor. *A Capital Punishment Anthology.* Cincinnati, OH: Anderson Publishing Co., 2001.

_____. *Death Penalty for Juveniles.* Bloomington, IN: Indiana University Press, 1987.

Torr, James D., and Laura K. Egendorf, Editors. *Problems of Death: Opposing Viewpoints.* San Diego, CA: Greenhaven Press, 2000.

Van den Haag, Ernest, and John P. Conrad. *The Death Penalty: A Debate.* Plenum Press, 1983.

Vila, Brian, and Cynthia Morris, Editors. *Capital Punishment in the United States: A Documentary History.* Westport, CT: Greenwood Publishing Group, 1997.

Williams, Mary E., Editor. *The Death Penalty: Opposing Viewpoints.* San Diego, CA: Greenhaven Press, 2002.

Winters, Paul, Editor. *The Death Penalty: Opposing Viewpoints.* San Diego, CA: Greenhaven Press, 1997.

Woodward, Bob, and Scott Armstrong. *The Brethren: Inside the Supreme Court.* New York, NY: Simon & Schuster, 1979.

Zimring, Franklin E., and Gordon Hawkins. *Capital Punishment and the American Agenda.* New York, NY: Cambridge University Press, 1986.

📖 EXCELLENT BOOKS ORDER FORM 📖
(Please xerox this form so it will be available to other readers.)

Please send the following books:
___ Death Penalty Decisions
___ Criminal Justice Decisions
___ Landmark American Speeches: The 17th & 18th Centuries
___ Landmark American Speeches: The 19th Century
___ Landmark American Speeches: The 20th Century
___ Landmark Decisions of the U.S. Supreme Court I
___ Landmark Decisions of the U.S. Supreme Court II
___ Landmark Decisions of the U.S. Supreme Court III
___ Landmark Decisions of the U.S. Supreme Court IV
___ Landmark Decisions of the U.S. Supreme Court V
___ Landmark Decisions of the U.S. Supreme Court VI
___ Freedom of Speech Decisions
___ Freedom of the Press Decisions
___ Freedom of Religion Decisions
___ Civil Rights Decisions: The 19th Century
___ Civil Rights Decisions: The 20th Century
___ Obscenity & Pornography Decisions
___ Schoolhouse Decisions
___ Life, Death, and the Law

- -

All Excellent Books are $19.95 each.
Order directly from us for a discount.
Add $2.00 shipping/handling for the first book
and $1.00 each for every other book ordered.

Name: _____

Organization: _____

Address: _____

E-mail: _____ Fax: _____

City: _____ State: _____ Zip: _____

Send your check or purchase order to:
Excellent Books, POB 131322, Carlsbad, CA 92013-1322;
Phone: **760-598-5069**; Fax: **240-218-7601**;
E-mail: **books@excellentbooks.com**;
or visit our website at **excellentbooks.com**